PASSING THROUGH TIME

Conversations with The Other Side

Nicole Suzanne Brown

Nicole Suzanne Brown
Passing through Time ...
Conversations with the other side.
By Nicole Suzanne Brown

Copyright © 2013 by Nicole Suzanne Brown
The moral rights of the author have been asserted. All rights reserved. No part of this book may be reproduced by any mechanical, photographic or electronic process, or in the form of a photographic recording; nor be stored in a retrieval system, transmitted or otherwise be copied for public or private use, other than for 'fair use' as brief quotations embodied in articles and reviews, without prior written permission of the publisher.

The author of this book does not dispense medical advice or prescribe the use of any technique as a form of treatment for physical or medical problems without the advice of a physician, either directly or indirectly.

The intent of the author is only to offer information of a general nature to help you in your quest for emotional and spiritual wellbeing. In the event you use any of the information in this book for yourself, which is your constitutional right, the author and the publisher assume no responsibility for your actions.
First Edition (Aust)
Published in Australia by Spiritual Wisdom Publishing
Nicole Suzanne Brown
Printed and bound by Book Pod Australia
Book design by Nicole Suzanne Brown © 2012 Nicole Suzanne Brown
National Library of Australia
ISBN 9780992273521

Books written by Nicole Suzanne Brown

Passing Through Time - Conversations With The Other Side

The Meaning of Feathers

The Meaning of Numbers

The Ultimate Waitress - How Life, The Universe & Everything is conspiring in your favour. (available 2019)

All books available on Epub, Kindle & Amazon

Testimonials

"Passing through Time is 'conversations with God' on a more intimate, realistic scale.
A lot of questions one might pose to God, or what we as mortal humans have perhaps considered inwardly, quietly to ourselves, Nicole openly asks her brother Jason, who has passed away in the prime of his life, he tells Nicole his own personal spiritual life experiences from 'the other side'. Nicole shows no fear in communicating with Jason, I would be a little uncomfortable in the same situation. However, she is perfectly comfortable sensing Jason's presence.
I love that Jason indicates to Nicole that life is the 'illusion', and death a kind of 'reality'. Regardless whether or not you believe in life after death, it's an interesting take on the philosophy of life.
Nicole cleverly interspersed the stark reality of Jason's sudden death via short takes from her Mum's diary. A humbling reminder of the other side of death, that whilst Jason is happy and content, those left behind are struggling. An enlightening read. Comforting and reassuring, no matter which side of the fence you sit on regarding your own personal beliefs on the big question, does life after death exist?"
Aishah Macgill
Co-founder of Australian Writers Rock
http://australianwritersrock.com

"Nicole Brown's book – "Passing through Time" is a beautiful breath of fresh Energy. It encapsulates Spiritual Philosophy and Spiritual Truths succinctly, and in such a way that really guides the reader through what may otherwise be very esoteric information. It was like re-connecting with a very wise friend. A Must-Read for anyone wanting to understand the Spiritual Dimensions of Life – this One and the Next!"
Donna Nelson
www.TheSpiritualAdventuresOf.com

"Passing through Time" written by Nicole Suzanne Brown is compelling, for anyone who has lost a loved one this throws light on a sensitive subject of death and yet Nicole's experience and illuminated interpretation gives great comfort for those who have had loved ones pass over. Not only does Nicole show a great depth of insight into the other dimensions that surround us in a new and inspired way this book is a rare find and a must read for anyone serious about their spiritual evolvement.
Jan-Marie Brooke
www.inspiredbrilliance.com.au

Dedication...
For Mum and Dad.
*For your love, truth,
friendship and memories
And
to those who remember.*

Acknowledgements

Thank you to our parents, for your love and honesty and allowing us both to walk tall and proud. We love you. You allowed us the freedom to find ourselves and laughed and cried with us with the memories that formed and shaped our lives. You are both extraordinary people. Thank you to Mum for sharing your journal entries with not only us, but the world.
Thank you to Gaylene. Your love shines through your smile. You are strong and beautiful. Never forget that. We love you. Thank you to our Grandparents: Iris & Jack Champion, Ray and Phyllis Brown.
Thanks to our family and friends for their love and support.
Many thanks go to all of Jason's friends throughout life. Jason wishes to personally thank all of those who laughed, danced, sang and loved with him, and for those who created memories in life that will never die.
A huge thanks to both Josie and Jean for your laughter and friendship.
But most importantly thank you to JASON for choosing us as a family to share your memories and dreams with, if only for a short time on Earth and now in eternity throughout all our lives. The days have been hard without you here, but your constant reminder that you are with us has brought such peace and understanding of the love we share.
We all love you Jay. I miss you physically, and hold the memories of us growing up together in my heart. Please help me to remember more. Thank you for being my Big Brother and my friend.
Nicole Suzanne Brown 2012

Acknowledgements 7

Introduction 10

First Conversation with Jason 12

Jason's Experience 14

Babies and Children 41

Suicide 47

Car Accident/Murder 51

Lost Souls 55

Past Lives 60

Leaving Time Behind 71

Love = Evolve 74

The ART of Purpose 78

The Purpose of Intentional Happiness. 81

The ART of Loving Purposefully 87

Change your Thoughts – Change your Life. 89

Self - Love 104

Self – Hope 107

Self-Joy 110

Do Angels Exist? 113

A Love Letter from a Son 120

Evolution 122

Self-Acceptance 131

The Inner-World 132

The GOD-Seed 137

Abundance 159

Weight Loss 164

Relationships 172

Meditation and Visualizations 176

Letting Go Visualization 180

A Question Asked 182

Prologue 183

Introduction

Jason was strong, fit and healthy. His death at age 29 of a heart attack on 20th December, 1998, came as a sudden shock to myself, my parents and his fiancé Gaylene (just engaged the day he died).
Through remembrance of his love for us all and mine for him, we began speaking to each other shortly after his death.

The following conversations of his adventures and remembrances of passing through time gave us all great comfort and helped us live through our loss and sadness.
He continues to communicate with me, and has taught me about what it is like to die, or as he chooses to call it 'Pass through Time'. Revelations of love, truth and peace-filled existence of the after-life is evident in his learning's and memories.
His and my only wish is for all of us not to fear 'death' or have fears for the loved ones that have passed 'before' us, but to remember and reconnect with each other through the love we share.
Nicole 2012

'I'm so happy now Mum. I've found my purpose'
Jason 16/12/98

First Conversation with Jason

The feelings of grief cannot be explained in layman's terms. For every single person it is an individual experience.
Some get angry, others remorseful. But, the most important thing for anyone, everyone, is that they feel every feeling to its full extent.
The first conversation I had with Jay was only days after he passed. Days for us, a lifetime for him. I was lying on his bed, listening to his favorite song, consumed with grief, confusion, heartbroken and lonely. I kept asking why? Why him, why now? When there were so many nasty people in the world, why 'take' him? I questioned GOD. I questioned every belief I had. And in that questioning with my own thoughts raging in my head, I heard him.
I will never publish the first conversation that we had. It was deeply personal. Messages for family and friends, loving memories that he had for each of us and only us. But in that first conversation we connected through time, through energy and through the love we have for each other. It's so important to be connected right now with the ones you love. Tell them how deeply you feel; tell them how grateful you are that they are who they are. Let them know that no matter what happens, not matter where you are in the world you *will* connect. Oceans apart or eons apart. You will always be connected.
Our family did that in the last phone call we had with Jay only hours before he passed.
We kept our promise.
We now hope we can teach you to make and keep yours. Nicole 2012.

My Son is dead.
My heart is breaking
and my Son is dead.
Journal entry - 21/12/98 Mum

Jason's Experience

Jay, what did dying feel like? So many people are so terrified of death. And I think it's the 'not knowing' that scares the crap out of everyone, even the most resilient.

For me personally, because everyone's experience of passing is different 'as is their life, so is their death' it was the most peaceful thing I have ever felt.

I remember laughing with Gaylene and making plans for our wedding and also our future. I remember lying there and talking with her with the lights out and I held her hand when I was falling asleep.

Then I remembered that I had this feeling of total peacefulness, it was like I was finally complete. I was grateful for all that struggle in my life to get me right here to this place right now. I knew where I was going in life, who I was, where I finally fitted in. I guess I had never really done that before - given thanks, been grateful, truly grateful for all that I have and don't have. I was grateful for the woman lying next to me, for Mum, Dad and you. My friends; for all that I received and had, I 'knew' who I was, finally. It's like I got it! I found the last piece of the puzzle, the clue to the riddle. I worked out the meaning of life. I remember saying 'If this is the happiest I am ever going to be'… Then …

… I was outside of myself, looking over Gaylene and I sleeping. I was lying on my stomach with my leg off to one side. There were all these colors around me. At first I thought they were all around me and then I noticed the colors were around everything.

It's amazing Nicole. Every time I breathed in, the colours changed to brighter vibrant colors.

Then every time I breathed out, they become pastel colors, still vibrant but not as bright. I remember lifting my hand up and watching the gold light like a wave, going not only around my hand, but through it as well. When I breathed in, things like objects became denser and when I breathed back out, they were shimmery, like a wave, like heat on a road. I guess that's how they explain energy. I remembered thinking this is what astral travelling is probably like.

I remember looking around the room and 'pushing' the colors with my hands. The colors moved and glided. They didn't crash into each other or become jagged or fragmented. They danced and gelled into each other, separating and then coming back together again. I'd never seen anything like it on Earth, but I just knew it was right. I wasn't scared or nervous I was excited and knew that that's how life was, always. That's how it is and we just don't see it.

I then looked more closely at my face. I remember thinking and feeling that it looked so grey and old, when all I felt was really young and fit. I guess you could say it was that I felt alive for the first time in my life. Really alive. Free. When I was looking at myself, it all began to change.

I realized when I breathed in I could see everything inside me, my lungs and my bones, my skeleton and my heart. I looked over at Gaylene and could see the same thing, her lungs going in and out with every breath she took and her heart beating. I smiled at her 'cause she looked so beautiful and peaceful. I looked back at myself again, lying there beside her and noticed something was different.

It took me a while I guess, looking back and forth from myself to Gaylene when it dawned on me. My lungs weren't moving and my heart wasn't beating like hers. It wasn't beating at all.

When I realized what that meant, I thought for a second that I should feel scared. I tried to and waited for the panic and fear to rise inside me...but it never came. I sat there for what seemed a long time, just looking at myself. Looking at my body, my face … And then I began to cry. Not because I was sad or scared, but because I wasn't. I knew what it all meant. I had died. It was sudden and not at all like I thought I would die. But I knew that I had left time behind for the last time. I was free. I didn't feel sad or frustrated or worthless. I didn't feel that struggle or fight to be good or funny or liked. I didn't feel anything negative at all. Just peaceful. Only peace.

After a while of sitting there, I wiped the tears from my eyes and looked down at them on my hands. My tears had now become gold light and energy. I remember thinking 'so that's what pure love looks like'.

I looked up and all the colors around me had become really bright and vibrated. Then through the colors came these people, or Beings of Light I suppose you would call them. And they were smiling at me. I remember looking at the Beings and shrugged my shoulders at them. Not like a 'well, what's next?' thing, but a 'So, this is it' thing.

They nodded as if they knew what I was thinking, and then they smiled at me and came closer.

It's funny to remember it now, but when you look at these Beings, their appearance changes to whatever or whoever you think about. The first thing I thought of was 'will I see Charlie Brown?' - our childhood dog. Isn't that funny? Then suddenly there he was, this being changed instantly into Charlie and came bounding up to me. I laughed and cried as I held him cause he was exactly how I remembered him. I then thought of White Feather - my spirit guide and another Being changed into him instantly.

He was a lot taller than I thought he would be and I guess the surprised look on my face is what made him laugh. As soon as we touched all the memories we had shared together over our lifetimes with him came flooding back, especially the times in this life, when I thought I had no-one, I could see now that he was there, standing behind me with his hand on my shoulder like he was just then.

I then thought of your spirit guide Nicole - Soaring Eagle and White Feather instantly changed his appearance to look like your guide, or how I imagined him to look - I'll talk to you more about that later. I thought of Mum's guide and again the face and the body of the Being changed. I must have thought something because I suddenly heard in my head that

'WE ARE ALL ONE - ALL PART OF EACH OTHER'

I thought of Grandad and Uncle Terry and Aunty Gloria and these Beings came through the colors and changed into them.

We all laughed and hugged each other. Uncle Terry looked really healthy, really young like I remembered him when we used to go fishing, or over at his place where we played pool. I must have started thinking of a lot of people then, because more and more Beings changed appearance to look like who I was thinking of. I even thought of Peter Allen - the singer - I don't know why; and he came in front of me. Now, HE'S a lot shorter than I thought he would be (laughs).

I then thought of you, Mum and Dad and looked back around to see myself lying there again. Beings changed into you, Mum and Dad and everyone I thought of that wasn't dead.

For a split second, I couldn't understand why.

Then as soon as I thought about it the answer came. 'There is no time'. Our lives truly are instant Nicole. What we see as a 'lifetime' really is just a blink of an eye or a single breath.

You and Mum and Dad and I all hugged and the memories of our lives together came flooding back, things I thought I had forgotten were instantly relived and we laughed and cried and I was once again thankful for having the life I had shared with you all.

I looked over at Gaylene and she began to wake up. I was concerned for her, although that 'feeling' didn't come over me - just the thought. I heard her telling me to roll over because she thought I was snoring. She then touched me and I saw my body go all stiff like an ironing board. It was like all my muscles went into spasm. She then jumped out of bed, ran over to turn on the light, and then was at my side rolling me over. She stepped back for a moment because my eyes were wide open. Then she put her head to my chest, checked if I was breathing and started CPR. Gaylene ran out of the room and called for an ambulance running back to check on me again and again trying CPR waiting for the ambulance to come. It was a strange feeling standing there viewing it all, watching her fight for my life. I thought that I would feel a pull emotionally or frightened or scared, but none of those feelings came. Then I realized something, and in that realization I turned next to me and a Being changed into Gaylene. She was with me, the energy of her, the energy of all that I loved about her was right here with me, witnessing it all with me, being there again for me. I thanked her for fighting for my life. I thanked her for loving me in my life, I thanked her for the person she was and thanked her for the memories I will always share and have with her.

Even though all of this was only just happening it was like it happened a long time ago, like when you stub your toe, or hit your thumb with a hammer. You remember it hurt, but that's all, you just remember. The pain doesn't come with those memories; you just remember that back then, it hurt. I don't want to dwell too much on my passing. I would rather, am here to, help you write, to remember with me, to learn and teach others about a more realistic experience of life on earth and on death, or as we like to call it 'Passing through Time'. Passing through time Nicole is an adventure, a mystery, an answer to the unknown that Western civilization (myself included), search for all their lives.

It is a plausible realization of the GOD-Force, GOD-Self in all of us. It is energy. It is pure love.

It is a fantastic area of life that we have closed the door on for so long; we forgot the great adventure it holds.

The realization of the Human Spirit is upon us. In your lifetime you will grasp your dreams, live your dreams in reality.

That is all we want, isn't it? Hopefully with these writings, people will begin to not search for the meaning of life but instead live and 'Be' their answer, only striving for them 'selves' the essence of who they really are.

I will tell you of great things, unbelievable sights and realizations as I come upon them and them upon me. This is my calling I have found my way.

Allow me to teach you to find yours.

Jason.

Jay, several times throughout these communications you have stated that 'when you take your first breath when you pass'. Does that mean you breathe after death? (I hear Jay breathe in and out and then 'feel' his shoulders shrug).

Yeah, I guess so. I never really thought about it. But then again, how many times on Earth do you actually 'think' about breathing. Remember, life is the illusion. Passing through time is the reality.

Can you feel?

Absolutely! The feelings are intensified to such a rapid vibration that all you do is feel. As I just explained, when communicating here and with you, feeling is everything. There is nothing separate or apart from that essence of energy.
I feel such love, more than I ever felt capable of or knew even existed. I feel peace, joy, excitement, anticipation, love for you all and also love for myself. Some here do feel anger or bitterness, but once they realize the energy that surrounds them, is them, they move rapidly into the energy of peace and love, that is just the energy of learning and remembrance.

Do you have a body that you are aware of?

When you pass, initially you have the 'thought' of the body that you did when you were on earth because it is comfortable and familiar.
Then when you become accustomed and used to the energy around you, you notice a change in your physical self. You become lighter and less dense in your energy. You become more luminescent with your surroundings.

You can call energy into your being until you realize that that's just what you are already - intellectual energy.

You begin to vibrate at a more rapid vibrational structure than you ever could on Earth. Therefore there is no need for such a dense vibrational form as a 'physical' body.

I can still be in the form of 'Jason' whenever I want or choose to be. The energy vibration of that intellect is just remembering or oscillating at a more defined or higher vibration molecularly. I like this form and these memories. I suppose you can say I'm just a mere shadow of my former self (laughs).

When I speak to you I am able to remember or re-invent the molecular structure of 'Jason' because you are used to that energy. You are comfortable with it. You are accustomed to it. You are also, importantly, connected to that particular vision of the energy I oscillate with. Now, by using the energy and becoming one with it, I am able, if I feel like it, to transcend my energy to an energy level outside of the physical form. We all do it, here and where you are. Although you call it 'dream state/ astral travel'. Same thing. Now, when we greet people who have passed and say their individual Prayer of Remembrance, we come in light form or 'light bodies'- bodies of light. That's what I saw when I passed and now I am one of them when other's pass. It seems to help the person passing through to 'remember' who they are and why they are.

The light that we emit is a remembrance and a resurgence of peace-filled love moving at a slightly higher vibration to that of Earth. You're kind of eased into the realization of remembrance. The energy then moves them to a particular energy- based realized form. We are all part of ourselves.

Have you any depth of the physical? Can you touch, smell etc?

Again, of course. Remember, the physical is the illusion. There on Earth, we use only 12% of our brain or intellect (some even less - laughs). The only reason that humans have the 'lower' intellect of remembrance is just that; they have forgotten their remembrance of the intellect.

Once humans establish a re-connection with their own vibration, their intellect then grows or oscillates at a higher more rapid energy. You are able to access more because, in remembrance, your intellect opens more to new ideas and growth 'spurts'. I am able to touch, smell, hear and see etc,. as I did on Earth, but again, at a more rapid molecular structure. I can also touch, hear, smell and see you in your own molecular structure. The touch you receive feels sometimes like a feather has brushed your face or hands.

Depending on the energy you are oscillating at, at a particular time, the touch may become stronger. Being in touch with your loved ones, connecting so strongly through thought, feeling, love and remembrance allows the boundaries to be lifted and the energy to flow freely. Your energy connecting with mine is through the energy of remembrance so you are able to 'receive' more senses. In those circumstances, the touch will become more direct - like someone poking you in the eye, sticking their finger in your ear, pulling your hair, or taps on the shoulder etc,.

It is in the energy of connection of remembrance that allows us all to communicate with each other, everywhere. Heaven literally on Earth.

Hopefully with our conversations, the people will begin to open their collective thoughts just enough to allow that to happen. More people especially in the western world seeking communication openly and lovingly will allow energy to move and evolve. Conflicts will lessen and love will shine through. Learning's of spirituality will be honored and taught from cradle to grave. Openly without fear, without boundaries. Eastern teachings know this, yet the western world is still lost, still confused, still feels alone and isolated.

Today James and I are going to pick up Jason's ashes and choose urns - one for us and one for Gaylene. I guess it is another step along the path of understanding and healing but it also wrenches my heart

As we are sitting at the table at the Crematorium - discussing ashes etc,. into my head comes ...
'I am not the body, Mum remember, I am not the body'.
And there it stays with me as I cling to the urn and go home.
Of course I know this. but the humanness remains
Journal Entry - 21/1/99 - Mum

Jay, how is this possible? How do you and I communicate? Can everyone do this? Connect with their loved ones that have passed? How can people communicate with their loved ones that have passed like you and I do? Can anyone do this? How long does it take to make contact?

They are always around you, for they never left you.
There is no need for time or separation. Thinking of your loved one draws the energy of who they are to you. Energy cannot help but be drawn to the same energy.

With passing you are pure energy, when thought of, you are pure energy, so with remembrance (remembering that loved one) you and they are 'drawn' to the same energy. Remember the memories, but on a deeper level. It is remembering the little things of that particular person that you hold dear. That enables contact.

Like when I remember your eyes 'bugging out' when you'd catch someone off guard with one of your practical jokes?

Exactly! Exactly that. Those memories are precious and dear to you and you alone. The way your loved one laughed, joked, cried, bit their lip when they were thinking etc, are all personal insights and memories of the ones you love.
Once you retain the energy of remembrance through those memories, you will attract a vibrational energy to that person which allows communication to then flow freely. You establish a desire and unconditional love/need for that particular person.

They are always around you, for they never left you.

Your loved ones that have passed have only chosen to evolve or move into different vibrational energy to the one you currently exist in. Imagine a world Nicole where what you and I are doing right now was normal?
Where Heaven and Earth co-exist. Where communication never has boundaries or distance. Where life never ends, just moves and grows, evolves and learns.

'I am with you, and all around you. Upturn a rock and you will find me. Split a piece of wood, and I will be there'
-Gospel of St Thomas

You are never separate or alone. This is so true when you are in the world as well as when you leave it. *Energy is everything.*
But the thing is Nicole when you do leave it, it is truly then that you appreciate your life and all those that loved you. In that instance when you pass you remember everything. From everything you and others have done and said but also your birth, your conception and beyond that.
Never EVER fear death. It is beautiful no matter how it came to be.
Remember when I told you that it's the ones that are still physical that only feel the pain? That is so true. It's all memories to us, we cannot re-create the hurt or pain, afterall where we are, is all just energy. Love at its purest form.

How do you communicate with me? How do the ones that have passed speak to those of us here on Earth?

Through thoughts: Same as you did when you were there.

You have a thought, and then using energy you 'voice' those thoughts to your loved ones.

Clear intention, focus.

Thinking of your loved one, picturing them and then focusing the energy of what you want to communicate to them, seeing them respond, being open, understanding. In the energy that we are in, you become aware that it is not necessary to 'voice' what it is you want to say. Actually, if you do, you seem to repeat yourself. Also, when voicing your thoughts in this vibration that I am in, the energy becomes less freeing. It seems that the monotone of the human voice vibrates at a far more dense energy, than actualizing thoughts.

You come to learn this in your own time, once you have passed. It's quite exhilarating really, because once you are aware of the non-speaking communication, you then - again in your own time of remembrance - realize it is not necessary to form a thought.
Your feelings shine through as bright as a ray of sunshine. Then you are able to communicate with your feelings 100%. The images projected towards - not at - another, seem brighter and more vivid. The energy level then escalates rapidly with each new remembrance. When you and I talk now Nicole, I transmit feelings, remembrances and images of learning's and miraculous events that I have been witness to. I use the energy as an intellect, not just a 'thing'. You are then able to receive those energy vibrations and understand, through your own gift of remembrance, what I am feeling.

You understand it through daydreams, and meditation, through déjà-vu and intuition. It's extraordinary to work out and such an amazing feeling when you do.

The gift of life is so precious, once understood and fully realized; it never ends, just grows, remembers and learns through its own intellect, memories and achievements.

I know you understand how happy I am. I want to share with you Mum and Dad and so many others, that I love what I'm seeing and feeling.

Being part of everything, every breath of life, every memory new and old. All I need for you to do is remember that feeling once you receive it and then visualize yourself being in that space hundreds of thousands of times over. That's how I can explain how it feels to be in this energy, this vibration. It's wonderful.

What can we say to people who say there is no such thing as 'the other side'?

Tell them I'll get to say "I told you so' when they see me. (laughs). If it's a cloudy night, aren't the stars still there? Isn't the moon still shining brightly? Just because you can't see it with your eyes doesn't mean it's not happening - you have to look with better eyes than that.

Be open to the miracle of never ending energy. Be open to the Universal knowledge that 'time' ends for no-one. Be open to accepting that which you don't understand and more harshly, stop being so judgmental on God's behalf. Because it IS no matter what you believe, think or have been taught.

Energy never never stops. It moves, forms, implodes, explodes and is in a constant state of change, whether we like it or not, whether we believe it or not, the only thing that is abundantly powerful is energy.

It's in all of us.
Three dimensional or otherwise.
We are part of everything and separate from nothing.

No matter how hard we try to believe our 'beliefs', no matter how hard we try to convince ourselves or others that there is only one way, one path, one answer, it is simply not the case, because that is 'limited' thought and the *Universe is limitless.*

Jay, why are people so scared of spirituality?

Because some people feel secure, feel safe in their little boxes. Some people feel safe with their blinders on. *And some people are so afraid of what they will discover inside themselves that they are quite content in being nonchalant about everything.* But remember this - *Never let their fear, their lack of inquisitiveness from destroying your faith, your hope in a better more loving spiritual world.*
Remember, you gravitate to what you vibrate towards. Those people that have blinders on will slowly disappear from your life 'till all you feel, all you see and all you interact with will be spiritual people.
People, who allow you to feel ridicule or feeling that you need to justify your beliefs, aren't worth playing with. Move away from them emotionally and you will feel so much better about yourself.

Jay, you said you saw Mum, Dad and myself when you first passed. How can that be when we are still living?

When you pass, you intellectually, through your own thoughts and feelings, draw things/energy to you that give you great comfort. In thinking about Mum, Dad and you and about how much I love you all, the energy of that love corresponded within itself and transformed into your own individual energies.

Now that I have seen so many events and wonderful scenes of passing, I now understand that what I actually did was draw to me your own individual and collective soul group, that which is all of you, sustains you, is apart from you but most importantly a part of you.

In that energy of you, I was able to identify, or more importantly, choose to see an individualized aspect that is identified as you. In doing this, I reconnected to the ultimate energy that is what makes you, you. This gave me great comfort and inner-peace knowing that we are never separate from one another, unobstructed by whatever distance we perceive there to be between us.

We are all part of each other.

Our memories, feelings, emotions, are all a part of the same soul 'psyche' you and I, we will always, always be with each other, never separate. Only our thoughts are keeping us apart.

Our judgment of 'here' and 'there' is the only thing, the *only thing* that separates us all from one another.

Jay, you talked about the Beings you first saw when you passed, about how they appeared to look, how you imagined they looked. What did you mean by that?

Over and over we are constantly reminded of choice. What we choose is what we live.

When the Beings of Light (I'm speaking past-tense now knowing that we are all indeed Beings of Light), came towards me, again the intellect reaches for something 'tangible', something it can grasp and understand, without causing any discomfort or attention to itself.

In doing this, I thought and felt about people and animals that I have/had a connection with. By 'Charlie Brown' (our first dog) first coming to me, it allowed me to gently understand the energy of intellect and choice.

Whereas if a Being of Light transformed into something or someone I had felt no connection with, naturally I would have been less self-assured and more self-anxious. Energy (Love) is an amazing thing. The sole purpose of teaching, learning and aspiring to the best of 'It's' ability is Love's desired destiny.

Energy doesn't conform, alienate, judge, or expect anything. The playfulness of 'energy' allows a gentler realization of all things here and on Earth.

Though while we are 'on' Earth, our thoughts and feelings, collectively and individually, become less playful in energy and more stringent with the acceptance of 'apart from', the energy that we accumulate around ourselves and oscillate within (ourselves) becomes again, playful.

Remember again, life (energy) is a wave, oscillating at any desired frequency you choose at all times.

Jay, how can people deal with grief? Sometimes, most times, it seems it feels all-consuming.

That's because it is. The energy of grief is a very complex and individualized, idealized energy. The people/beings who are going through the grieving structures, are more so in Earth than the people walking on it. What I mean is, everything seems raw and uncluttered. You no longer float along...You notice all things, every little thing, because you feel maybe, just maybe, in noticing those 'little things', they may be the answer or reason for all of what you are going through.

Remember, you never get over grief, but you do get through it. Allowing yourself to feel all your emotions without restrictions or judgment is so very important.

If you are angry, get angry for as long as it takes until you feel the anger subside. If you are fragile and emotional, get emotional, be fragile. Do not feel you have to dust yourself off and keep 'plodding through' hoping that one day it will all be over.

It won't be.

Allow yourself the choice to get though it - not over it.

Speaking with people who are going through the grieving structure is so important. For they are honest and gentle and will fully understand what you are living with and through.

Try not to upset yourself over people who tell you that life goes on and that time heals all wounds. They are at a loss for words about your grief and feel they are doing the right thing by you, but most importantly, by themselves. Normally in situations like that, they naturally are feeling somewhat relieved that what you are going through, is not happening to them.

Allow yourself as much time as you need. You are forever changed because of this grief and the memories of loss. Everybody lives through grief in their own individual way. Allow others to grieve in their own way. Be there for them, without the need to smother them with half truths and overprotection.

You are forever changed and your strength is forever strong. There are no antidotes for grief; only simply living each minute at a time. Breathing in and out (consciously) and knowing that your loved one, who you are grieving for, is beside you, filling your intellect with joyful memories and such love that they have for you.

I love you so much.

Jay, yesterday you have been gone (physically) for two months. Please tell me it gets easier to live with, or through.
It does Nicole. Remember that by allowing yourself the need to grieve also allows the painful memories of your loss to diminish and before long the memories of your love for me will shine through. Never fear that I will leave you. I am more so a part of you now, more than ever.
Please believe that.

I do. It's just hard, that's all.

I understand.

Jay, people say that if we do not grieve and then let go, that that person who has passed will forever be Earth bound. Is that true?

Nah. It's crap. Don't get me wrong - if people want to believe that, more power to them. But here, now, we (you and I) are giving people the realistic viewpoints of passing, with non-judgment and no expectations.

Know this, remember this; No-one ever has the power to do something to you or make you do something that you do not want to do.
I
f the Being who passed has people grieving their loss so distraughtly, so emotionally, they will always be by their side. Because of course, if someone loves you so unconditionally, loves you fully, you want to be with them and near them.

The Earth is so full of restricted views and judgments of other's emotional well-being, it's time for a change.

Know this, as I have said before, whenever, *whenever*, you think of a person who has passed, their energy surrounds you instantaneously. No exceptions.

It cannot help but be. Like attracts like. The pure energy of who they are and why they are, enables them to be apart from yet a part of all energy. Once you remember them vividly and with such love and compassion, they are with you, around, above, below and within you, showering you with such love and memories. It is a truly blessed event in all of life.
And so, to answer your question: No; no-one is Earth bound, except the people who think they are just the body and they are still on Earth.

Remember, the instant you breathe your first breath as you pass you are free. Free of restrictions, judgments, expectations. There are no rules here. It is true what they say 'The rules are that there are no rules'. A contradiction yes, but a fact nevertheless.

Jay, I remember a dream I had a few weeks after you passed. It was awful - you were so angry and violent and you were saying 'why have you done this to me?' I woke up screaming - why would I dream something like that about you?

You were so scared that one day you would forget me, forget what I looked like, how I felt, smelt, laughed that you created energy around you that night that your subconscious picked up as angry and violent - but most of all Nicole those words, that was you - those were your words coming out of my mouth in that dream.

You were so angry at God for taking me - you saw it as unfair, that it was a mistake, that something you did you were getting punished for.
You had and have every right to be of course - remember there are 'stages' of grieving - you just got to the pissed off at God part pretty quickly.

(laughs - true)

..after that dream didn't we first connect? And there was no fear or apprehension from you, just acceptance and love. That's what you needed to feel at the time to get through what you were going through.

Jay, what do Fathers tell you after they have passed, about their sons?

'I should have said I love you'. 'I should have held him more and touched him more'.
It's so difficult for me still to this day, to express emotions and it's an emotional link that they all have with their fathers. That's one vibrational rate that is interesting to watch - the emotional link of the male human being. We are all such amazing thinkers and inventors and providers but as communicators? (laughs)
Some have crossed the bridge but until men's groups become predominate in adulthood it will continue to struggle. It's a slower evolution that's for sure (laughs again). The younger males have it with scouts and rovers etc, but adult male groups are few and far between unless you count professional sporting teams - but they are a whole other evolution, very limited and so steeped in tradition and chauvinism.

Once adult male groups become the norm, evolution will take a huge step forward. But until men see that they can actually question their fathers' beliefs, attitudes and rules to live by without ridicule, pain and isolation they as a race will continue to evolve at a more mediocre vibrational rate. They will get there; just when the shift will happen is the mystery.

Jay why does it hurt so much, even when we do remember that those that have passed are still with us?

It's the human emotion Nicole. You miss the physical, which is completely natural. If you did not feel loss, or heartache, you would not fully recognize the energy of complete love. Try never to regret. All that was said and done was as it should be. And of course, all that wasn't said and done, is as it should be also.
I know that so much has happened in your life as well as mine. You may not see it yet, but you've pushed through a lot of fears and barriers. I miss you all physically and my heart aches as yours does. I feel your pain and anguish.

(I feel like Jay is talking to all of us - Mum, Dad, Gaylene and myself)

I am. It's just that I can speak through you more clearly. I trust your instincts and your writing and we both know that this is going further than family and friends.
I feel it is important to note here that Jay wants to tell families and loved ones of the people who passed, about the colors and beauty that is all around them, eternally, sharing its love and acceptance of their soul's energy with them.
I smile every time I think of Jay in that beauty.
The colors I saw and continue to see since I passed, become brighter as I breathe in, more-so than when I breathe out.

But this is not to say that one is more important than the other - just different that's all. When I noticed the colors becoming more vibrant, I was aware of my thoughts changing to a higher frequency. I was able to access more information - more memories. At first they were my own, but once I relaxed with the feelings of the colors, I was aware of collective memories - even yours.

I have later remembered that we are all one thought - one collective feeling - that ebbs and flows, that moves in and out like a wave of energy. I have become accustomed to the notion of high proportionate energy. That energy is how we become sustainable in our own energy field.

I'll try to explain it a better way. I'll use the example of a drop of blood. Some people may notice redness of the color, others may notice the roundness of the blood. But once you look closer, say under a microscope, you become aware of millions and millions of tiny fragmentations of that same drop of blood. It's like a little city - quite fascinating to view.

That's how I view our world. It is the energy of color which sustains us. It is the very life we breathe. Once I became aware of the colors not only around me but flowing through me as well, I was able to grasp a more direct awareness of our intellect, our collective idealism of reality. Basically, life is a wave.

Our life seems to jut out or become stagnant with energy but in all sincerity this is not the case. Even when you feel you have gone nowhere in your life, you have actually moved with the collective consciousness to where you need to be at such a rapid movement of time, that you feel no movement at all. This is how life (or energy) escalates.

This is true of the time continuum. You move through space and time rapidly, only you don't seem aware of it. You feel you are going at a snail's pace.

I have learnt further of this. Like putting blood under a microscope, we have this need to dissect life to see if anything else exists, apart from ourselves.

This is why we chose/choose the human form. We all seem, on the surface, to have separate lives, names, intellects and experiences, but these all sum up the collective experience of the whole.

What made us is us. What moves us is us. What drives us is us - and that us can be summed up in one word, which means millions of different things - LOVE. Love is energy. Love is us.

An interesting factor of the word Love is that you can use nearly every letter twice and you come up with the answer to life. Why we are.

When people are dying, not fully passed yet, how can we ease their fear?

Speak of your love for them. Remind them of what I have spoken of. Allow them their choice. It is what they need to experience before passing. It is their plan. Their Universe is conducted in how they choose to view it. As in life, in death.

Allow yourself to forgive and allow them to forgive themselves too. Speak gently of what they will witness - extraordinary sights and sounds.

Allow them the remembrance of life being the illusion.

Allow them their own energy, for you will never know (unless you have the gift of remembrance already recognized within yourself), what they are thinking and feeling. Speak fondly of the ones who have passed before them.

Speak of vivid colors and extraordinary love of self and themselves.

Passing through Time (conversations with the other side) Nicole Suzanne Brown

There is a paragraph of words that you can say for yourself and also for the one who is passing if you choose to.

It is words of remembrance. Remembrance of the love you shared and gave to one another.

It is beautiful, as it is gentle.

WORDS OF REMEMBRANCE

And as you pass through time remember us, as we will you.
Keep the memories alive,
of your love, your humour, your life as we will live fully with
the knowledge of
your life and the love you gave. Help us to remember our
own divinity, with no judgment to ourselves or another.
Allow us the freedom to miss you and in doing so we will begin to remember that you never leave us. Visit us frequently in our memories, our dreams and guide us to our full knowledge of who we are and why we are. We now acknowledge and remember fully that you are not apart from us, but a part of us.
You live in us, as we in you.
We love you.
For we remember the divine plan. In letting go, we receive.
In loving, we are loved.

Babies and Children

Jay, what about babies and children, do they have the same experience of passing as you?

Oh! Theirs is a wonderful experience because they still have the full realization of who they are and why they are. The colors dance and laugh around them and they laugh and embrace all who are remembered. It is such a great vibrational structure to be a part of that I choose to witness every one that I can. Do not feel desperate sadness for a young child that passes, for they are gifted souls awakened in the knowledge of love and remembrance.

What can bring the parents of these children and babies comfort through their grief, if anything?

Allowing the realization to form within themselves about the concept of choice. Death at any age or stage through life is hard, if you think of it in purely human terms. Allowing themselves to remember the divine plan and begin to search and grow through their own memories and the love of their child.
Speak with your child - Creative drawing is also an excellent way to work through the grieving process. Notice how, by using colored pencils or paints, the colors become stronger, more distinctive and vibrant, when the energy of your child is near.
Become receptive in your thought patterns.
Notice if any of their favorite songs play through your mind. And if they do, when they do, sing along with them. It gives them great excitement having you be in 'sync' with them.

Acknowledge their true gift of innocence. If you hear small bells or lilting music, that is your child through their own way, contacting you and letting you know that they are happy, healthy and free.

Remember, and this is most important. You never get over grief But you do get through it.

Do children and babies continue to grow as they would on Earth, even after they pass?

There is no need for growth of the physical body once you pass. That is a vibrational structure that occurs only in the physical energy. Therefore, when parents see their child through visions or dreams and their child has grown physically, it shows that the human intellect owns a comfortable idealism of the hereafter.

Let me explain - normally, but not in all cases, after some years have passed, the parents will dream of their child with the equivalent number of years on in their physical appearance I.e. if the child passed at age 3 and three years later you dream of your child at age 6, this allows the physical yearning of the child to dissipate as it shows your child is happy and healthy.

It calms you, allowing you to move into a higher awareness because you know, or now remember and have knowledge of your child as safe, happy and willing to communicate with you through your dreams.

Remember again - AS IN LIFE, IN DEATH.

It is all choice. Choice of the intellect, choice of the collective consciousness divine plan. Nothing is right or wrong. Just different.

All is energy. All is love. All is One, is One.

Jay, what about miscarriages? Why do they happen and sometimes repeatedly to the same person?

The conception and birthing process is such an intricate structure of energy's experience. So many times, if a miscarriage occurs it is the human body's way of releasing and clearing blocked energy.

This is not to say that the baby is blocked energy, but in most cases, the energy of the human body that is carrying the baby subconsciously is renewing the energy of its life. 90% of cases, after a miscarriage has occurred, the life of that woman changes its vibrational structure. Many insights and fears are faced in one's life when miscarriage occurs. Miscarriage is the body's natural way of renewing the primal instinct of that person and or relationship.

The body of the woman is forever changed because once conception is maintained, the body's vibration is heightened, allowing insights. The true feminine aspect of compassion and unity is then transfixed in that person's life. Please remember, as hard as it sometimes seems, everything is as it should be.
Once the body's energy is righted, cleaned and cleared, then the birthing structure will evolve to full term. In many cases after the miscarriage has occurred, the conception of the Being was not planned by the woman or man.

Many couples then have to question themselves as to the idea of parenting and raising a child in their lives. Some questions you could both, women and men, ask yourselves are:

1. Are we secure in our feelings for one another?
2. Is our relationship strong and as it should be, now?
3. Are we in the right space for parenthood?
4. Will our relationship be as strong in 2 weeks, 2 months, and years on?

After miscarriage occurs, the experience enables you, both women and men, to look back on the situation and realize that a baby at that time would not have been appropriate in their lives.
Once the woman and man heighten the molecular level of both their bodies and lives, the conception and a full term structure of the birth occurs. Remembering also like attracts like. The energy that both their bodies are sustaining and oscillating at is a very intricate part of the overall conception. The growing of the baby is an amazing structure to witness. Not only is the baby's own energy oscillating, evolving and transforming the energy of itself to shape and mould its physical appearance, but also the thoughts and feelings and beliefs of the woman and man and their environment also enables the child to form into a physical version of what the energy is oscillating and evolving to.
In other words, energy in its purest form - being the soul - evolves and oscillates at a molecular structure which corresponds to the vibration of that soul's thoughts and feelings.

Ok, I understand that, but now that you have said that *'after conception the being has thoughts and feelings and also evolves due to the woman and man's thoughts and feelings'*.

What about abortion? Knowing now, that the child is indeed alive, doesn't that protest strongly against aborting such a being?

Again, as I just said, the child is oscillating and evolving at its own vibrational structure as are the parents of the child. The divine plan of the collective consciousness and more so of the individualized divine plan is pure and evolving at all times. The child, knowing its own divine plan and that of the woman and the man, has chosen that particular structure of 'abortion' for its own experience.

With the experience of abortion, the energy of the child has had the unique experience of conception knowing it will not experience the physical structure of life. Of course, if more than one abortion occurs and that woman's body remains in the vibrational structure of abortion, she must look within and begin to take responsibility for her life and her actions.

Again, miscarriage is the child's natural way of evolving and or oscillating with itself and the energy of conception, without the structure of the physical. Once all the energies child, Mother, Father - are oscillating at the same vibration then the process from conception to physical structure is complete.

The realization of his death is more real every day and our lives will never be the same. Journal Entry - 27/1/99 Mum

Suicide

Jay, what about suicide? Why do people choose to take their own life?

The act of suicide is a hard one to explain in 'earthly' terms; because it always seems to be fuelled by a sheer act of desperation or anguish. We must all remember the choices we make and made. Nothing is wrong or bad, just vibrates or for want of a better word, 'moves' in a different vibrational energy field.

Suicide, once committed, has one large advantage. It enables the ones' who are left behind to finally open up and communicate about their thoughts and feelings.
Nearly all people, who are left with the memory of someone who has committed suicide, are left with the feelings of 'why?' And when those feelings surface, you can step back from the situation and see a change in yourself through someone else's actions.
You begin to question how you feel. Are you happy? If not, how can you change the situation you are in? And believe me, you begin to work darn hard at changing your current vibrational energy to one that feels 'home' to you. You may feel you need to change your attitudes and beliefs about your own life and about all those around you. Judgment recedes, and Love steps in. You no longer will take anything for granted - life, loved ones, friends etc, - because you acknowledge that you can move through the situation without feeling drastically aware that there is no way out.

Your communication level will step into a new vibrational energy once you acknowledge your loss and hurt and move through to the energy of understanding the collective consciousness of choice.

Many people feel angry or bitter at the person who has committed the act of suicide because they feel that person had everything to live for.

But you see it all comes down to choice.

Choosing to take your own life is an intricate part of taking responsibility for one's own actions. When someone you love suicides, the main thing you must do for yourself is forgive yourself. Nothing you could have said or done would have changed the outcome of that person's life because it was *their* life plan.

I acknowledge that this is hard for some to comprehend, but I have spoken to many here who have committed the act of suicide (in one form or another) and all say the same thing.

They felt they no longer belonged in this world. This is not to say that they didn't acknowledge the love of family, friends and loved ones. It was just time to come home.

Those people who have committed the act of suicide, feel or felt as I did. With the first breath they took when they passed, they remembered who they were and why they were. They are free; they are happy and pure and remember the GOD-seed that was planted before time began.

There is no guilt, anguish or foreboding here only an immense 'feeling' of pure love.

Your being is so peaceful, it literally is 'peace filled'.

All people I have witnessed during and after the act of suicide, acknowledge the anguish in their loved ones' hearts, but wish for their loved ones to learn from their act and move on to a vibrational energy the feels 'home' to them personally.

The energy of forgiveness is achieved through the Earth's energy vibrational rotation field.

All is one, is one.

Suicide is one of the, (if not the) hardest subjects to broach because everybody has a different opinion (or judgment of) the act itself.

But remember this - With love, pain heals.

With remembrance, hearts embrace with the energy of memories and anguish will be no more.

Teach yourself to speak freely and honestly with a gentleness that touches the hearts of all you come across.

Teach your children to not be ashamed of their feelings and thoughts. Allow them the honest gift of communication.

After the act of suicide and once the person has the energy vibration of peace-filled pure love (which is instant) flow through them, they are enriched with a deep sense of purpose. They will help you when and if you are ready to learn, to remember, to feel fully, to communicate readily and to accept responsibility for every choice you make - from feeding the dog, to cutting someone off in front of you when driving.

It is all choice. Pure and simple. Nothing in energy is wrong, bad, evil or sinful. As well as nothing and everything is right, good, higher or better. It is only energy … Only Love. And the only thing, the only thing that will make those words a fact is the act of judgment.

Choose love, laughter and happiness with every breath you take.

At the beginning is this cocoon-like feeling - of being here, but not here - of feeling everything and also, feeling nothing.

I had always marveled at the strength of families at funerals - but I understand now that it is our God-Self's protective bubble that we are in.

Journal Entry - 21/1/99 Mum

Car Accident/Murder

People that are murdered or in car accidents, do they see what you saw? Do they feel pain, fear etc, before they die?

The ones that I have witnessed, experienced part of what I experienced. What I mean by 'part of' is, they all seem to be in a form of dimensional protection bubble.
They witness what is happening to their bodies, but are no longer feeling the emotion of what is happening to them. Maybe that's what I was in too, I just wasn't aware of the dimensional vibration that forms around people at their passing.
It also depends on your experience of choice.
You can choose to not witness the event and therefore you don't. Or you can choose to witness the event. The choice is yours.
Remember, the first thing you feel as you pass, is peaceful, pure love energy, through and around your body. There is no longer fear, or feelings of being isolated and alone. You are in complete control. You see, feel, hear what you choose to.
You are instantly aware of who you are and why you are. Sure you can go through the illusional dimensions of unworthiness and fear, it is your choice.
As in life, in death.

Always remember that. I cannot stress that enough.

AS IN LIFE, IN DEATH.

What you think, feel in life, you will think and feel in death. What you perceive as good and bad, right and wrong in life, you will experience in death.

In communicating with you, the energy of 'here' vs 'there' is lessened and just becomes 'now'. Those that pass through no longer fear, but accept. They no longer analyze but believe in faith.

Death is not the illusion: Life is.

The only reality is that of the energy of passing. There is no sorrow, anger, hatred, bigotry, condemnation, isolation or feelings of solitude, reprimand or judgment.
There is only love.
Remember the feelings of when you first realized you were 'in love'?
That is the energy that surrounds us here. It can surround you too, if you choose.
Become in the moment. Allow every feeling to flow through you, not control you.
Remember the feelings of duality, the feeling of 'being at one' with a person. Remember the greatest joy in your life and carry 'the energy' of that moment with you, every day and forever.
I would like to share with you a prayer that Mikail (Archangel Michael), myself and others say when we greet beings who first pass through time.

Holy Spirit
Who is within us
Holy be this day.
In the kingdom you come as your will is done on Earth as it is in Heaven.
Have this day, your remembrance
And forgive yourself, as you forgave those with judgment toward you
Release us from such judgment.
For thy is the kingdom
Your Power,
Your Glory
For ever remembered,
As one, is one.

That's beautiful Jay. It's very special. Thank you for remembering, for sharing with me and others' your journey, your adventure, your love and your remembrance. I love you. You are such an incredible person.

As are you. Remember this always. I have the words to say, you know how to say them. Remember our emails? I hold that as a special memory because it reminded me about our divine plan.

Which is? What do you mean by our?

The divine plan of our two souls was to meet in life, forgive each other of wrong doings, find love in opposites and non-judgment and establish a connection so strong in our hearts that it surpasses all time. For our learning that all IS, and our teachings are of the same.

You spoke of Mikail again. Do you not see others, or just choose to hang around him?

Mikail laughed hard when you chose the words 'hang around'. There are others sure, but I acknowledge that All is One, is One and I found great comfort when I was in Earth's dimension with the movie "Michael" so I find comfort and a strong bond with Mikail here.
There are no levels here. I have not come across any energy vibrational where I was not allowed or permitted to go or bear witness to.
There is no need to be healed or search for a light - go towards a light or look for a light. Light is energy. We are energy. We are the light.

There is healing energy. All souls are pure, full of light and love and the remembrance of that comes to you with your first breath of passing. It cannot do otherwise. Your mind expands and escalates at such a rapid rate that it is indeed mind-blowing.

Lost Souls

Is there such a thing as a lost soul?

If you want there to be.

What do you mean by 'want there to be'?

Remember, choice. There are lost souls if you want there to be. If you choose to have lost souls around you or you just have the notion that there is a possibility of such a thing, there will be. It is your choice. With all the love, prayers, memories and remembrances that someone who has passed receives from the loved ones on earth, they feel that love and with that, they acknowledge who they are and why they are with their first breath of passing.

Now if they themselves choose to feel nothing and go nowhere, or are in limbo for all eternity, that is what they will receive until they choose something different. It is all a matter of choice. For those on Earth who believe in lost souls, they create the energy of a vibration that lives up to their experiences. If they expect to feel, see, hear an entity (evil or otherwise), they have chosen to focus on one part of that energy that will correspond with their particular thought process.

Humans have a desire (which is in-built in their psyche) to 'save' someone. It is classed as a heroic gesture of ultimate morality. And so be it, if that's what you choose. There is no right or wrong. Only CHOICE.

Also, while we are on the subject, there is no need to 'send' people towards the 'light'. Here, there is always light for we are as our surroundings. If you still feel there is a 'lost soul or entity' near you, ask yourself the following questions with love:

What part of me needs to be saved?
or
Have I received and remembered balance in my life?

The latter refers to people who only 'choose' to see the more negative side of life, such as mixed emotions, feelings of loneliness and isolation. They are calling forth the light (energy) because they need the rejogging of remembrance of who they are and why they are.

Is there such a thing as a lost soul or ghosts? Can people who pass become lost? Do you send people to the light?

Now I need to clarify something. There have been many who have witnessed 'spirit' and seen it as malevolent, 'a haunting', evil etc,. This is simply not the case. Someone who lives solely in the 3rd dimensions would truly sense a 'presence' and deem it as malice. Energy is energy; it's only the words we use that begin to separate or for want of a better word 'label' that energy which is 'felt'.
Many people would love to see spirit or hear their loved one but then have a fear of the unknown linked subconsciously with that urgency. So as soon as it is seen and or felt, apprehension wells inside of them and clouds their judgment of what was just witnessed. They then labeled the energy as malice, evil and or demonic, because after all, people don't ever like feeling pain and will try to avoid it at all costs.

Now, energy gives you exactly what you feel you deserve right? So doesn't it make sense that when someone is automatically 'scared', 'afraid', or 'fearful' of seeing spirit that they get exactly what they thought? They get to experience first-hand those feelings they have sent out to the Universe to receive. Now, if they were to relax, to be open to the wondrous miracle of love, God, energy or whatever you wish to label it as, what 'feelings' do you think you will feel?

Energy is energy. You can use fancy words to label and confuse others with, but it all comes down to that. Energy is energy.

Some people would love to be in contact with their loved ones that have passed. We hear their prayers every day. But we also feel their energy and for those people with apprehension or fear linked to it or worse yet, guilt or anger towards the person who passed, we stand back and shower them with as much love as they will allow themselves to receive.

Slowly, with that energy surrounding them they accept and their fear and apprehension is diminished more and more until we can truly show our true forms - that of energy, love and acceptance.

The dream state is the easiest way for us to be in contact with you for your subconscious mind is open, your conscious mind in sleep-state and you do not stop and rationalize or over-analyze what is happening.

Jay you say there is no malice or evil energy, but what about when you walk in a room and feel scared or sense a dangerous situation? Isn't that picking up or intuitively feeling a vibe of badness?

You just answered your own question with the words you chose Nicole - 'feel scared' 'sensed danger' 'intuitive feelings'.

You gravitate towards that which you create. Energy attracts energy.

If you walked into a room where you 'felt peaceful' 'felt at home' was 'relaxed' do you automatically come to a conclusion that there is an angelic loving energy in there with you?

no

Yet, when you 'feel scared' etc, you automatically conclude there are 'bad vibes' or 'evil presences'. When in rooms or situations like that what normally happens?

I leave

Even when others have been there, or chose to stay?

yes

Do you not think it's only because the energy in that situation or room wasn't vibrating at the same rate as yours so you felt compelled to leave, to move into a vibrational that matched your own?

Mum just read what you have told me - she told me a story of when she and Dad went to the Vietnam Vets meeting and they both felt apprehension when they entered the room - she immediately filled the room with love and light and felt better.

Ok. Classic example, what she actually did was eliminate her fear or apprehension by calming her thoughts and focusing on positive imagery - the rooms' vibration remained the same - her energy changed to that beyond the fear, towards acceptance.
Remember there is no need to 'fill' a room with light, or send someone who passed 'to the light'.

Energy is light, even in the blackest of black holes there is light. For light is energy and vice versa.

But Mum subconsciously did the right thing for herself. It's what you all should do in situations where you feel afraid or apprehensive. Positive imagery is one of the greatest ways to enhance a situation into a positive outcome.

To vibrate at a faster vibration, to move beyond the fear and the apprehension and just be in the state of love and peacefulness.

Past Lives

Jay, is there such a thing as a past life?

Not in the sense that human beings perceive. There is no past and no future. There is only now - this instant. Therefore, there are no past lives.

Everything, everything is happening simultaneously.

When people view or have visions of past lives, they have raised their own Vibrational Molecular Structure to a degree where they can view there soul's progress.

Let me explain it this way. You're soul surrounds your body; it does not live in or is not surrounded by your body. The soul is a multi-dimensional intellectual energy - therefore many 'parts' make up the whole.

When you have viewed or had visions of a past incarnation, you (individually as well as collectively), have placed yourself into the energy of all-knowing and allremembering. When you view these lives, it feels as if you are really there. In other words it feels 'real'.

That is because it is. It is all happening now. You have just moved your personal energy to blend with the collective consciousness as well as the Universal consciousness, to enable you - your 'self'- to reconnect with other parts of your divine self. The Vibrational Molecular Structure of the human intellect or collective consciousness views life in linear time.

The energy of GOD-Force of Remembrance oscillates - not just from left to right, but left, right, up and down. In the energy of learning, there are points of remembrance that oscillate at a higher frequency than other points.

When all the points click together and sustain themselves in a vibrational divinity of remembrance, the energy of remembrance is thrust into a higher vibrational structure.

For example, instead of 'viewing time' as linear -

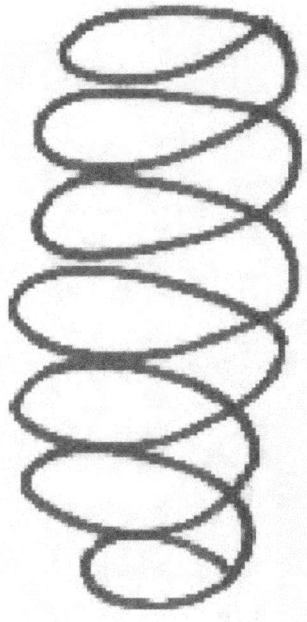

72

The energy vibration evolves in wave-like or spring-like fashion - side-on, the energy vibration would appear like multi dimensional energy.

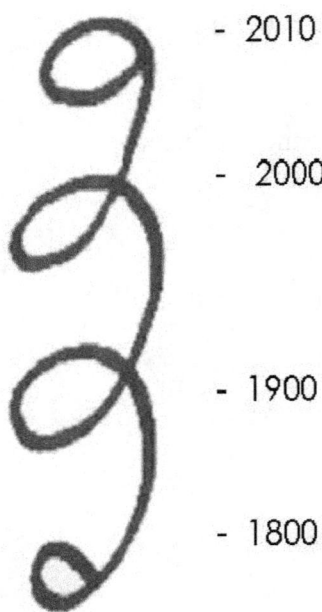

Side-on – the energy vibration would appear like this.
Multi-dimensional Energy

Energy is a never-ending oscillation (like an infinity sign).

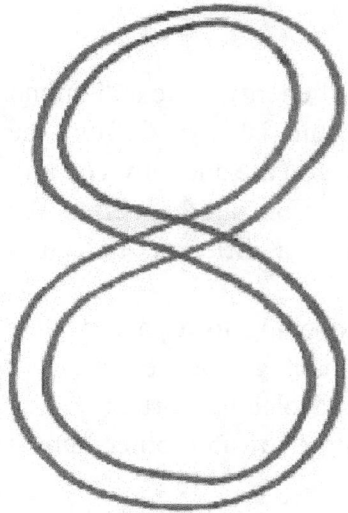

Remember, what we view as past history and past centuries is actually the collective consciousness idealism of such lessons and events taking place right 'now'. We have moved in Vibrational Molecular Structure but time (as humans understand it), does not exist.

On Earth, time is viewed as moving from second to second, minute to minute, hour to hour and so on. In that movement, we assume that there has to have been a past (looking back) and a future (looking forward).

Once we, as collective and individualized consciousness remember that energy oscillates as waves or currents and not back and forth, we will all move into the Vibrational Molecular Structure of no-time.

Therefor when you view yourself as a maiden in Celtic dress amidst the scenery of the Scottish Isles (or any other 'past life' vision), ask yourself these questions:

In this space now, do I remember who I am and why I am? What is my space of all-knowing, what is my next remembrance of my 'divine plan?'

And finally –

Am I being all that I can be right now?

Your soul is a multi-dimensional facet of energy. Like a diamond with its many cuts and facets, your soul is created from the Vibrational Molecular Structure of who you are and why you are. In there being no time, all your soul's lessons are happening (or for a better understanding, evolving) at a different molecular structure all at the same time.

This means that everything that is happening to a part of your soul personality is happening and shaping your evolvement through your individualized Vibrational Molecular Structure.

This is how you form opinions, gravitate towards other human beings, choose your lessons, and so on.

When you view or have a vision of a different time and place, it is explained by all the vibrational energy that is you (made of you and from you) and evolves to exactly the same vibrational level which causes your intellect to expand into remembrance.

Your current stage of evolvement dictates what insights you view and witness and what degree of feeling and memories you access.

For a Soul whose evolvement is at a less rapid Vibrational Molecular Structure their multi-dimensional core may look like this –

- Remembering who you are and why you are.

- Remembering who you are and why you are

- Remembering who you are and why you are

- Remembering who you are and why you are

As shown above, whenever the vibrational structure of your various soul parts meet or join, a higher vibration is produced, which results in your soul's learning or remembrance. You can access who you are and why you are at an intellectual level of evolvement.

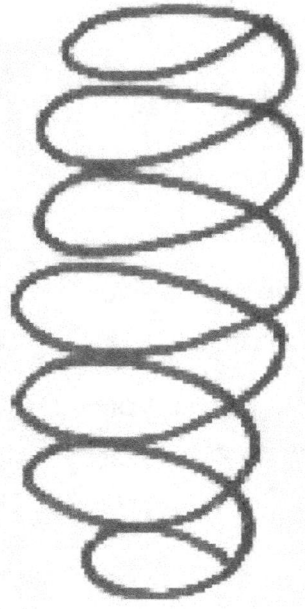

If a being has accessed more information about who they are and why they are their core path my look as follows:

The more your remembrance is obtained by searching and questioning yourself, the more information or remembrances occur.

Finally, when a Soul has brought through the energy of total knowing and total remembrance, their core path my look like

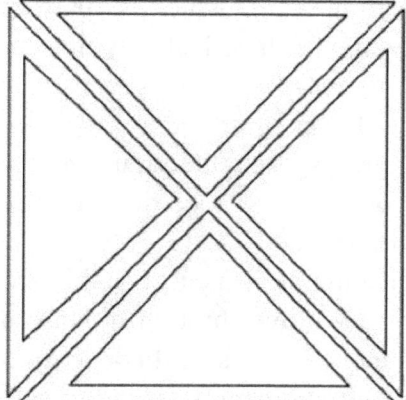

In early evolvement, the soul finds its life filled with chance meetings, coincidences and feelings of déjà vu.

However, once a soul has accessed the intellectual Vibrational Molecular Structure of who they are and why they are, they then see those 'coincidences' and 'chances' as a pathway to higher learning.

They understand the benefit and significance in taking notice of those particular signs or chance meetings by utilizing and accessing the information fully, both collectively and individually. They no longer find life a struggle, but use it to their own evolvement, through nonjudgment and living in the energy of no-expectations.

Jay, what is a soul group and how do we contact them?

Your soul group is what identifies you to the outside world. It is the energy or group that oscillates at the Vibrational Molecular Structure of gentle remembrance and accelerated learning.

There are many parts of a soul group - that which is apart from you and that which is a part of you, which collectively makes up the whole experience of you.

Remember, no energy is higher or lower - just energy.

The integral part of your soul group, your individualized soul group, is made up of, or evolves at a specific vibrational structure of 'who you are and why you are'.

You, as a GOD-Seed soul, are in complete unison with this group or energy. It is how you oscillate - move through dimensional vibrations to learn, teach and remember. It is in this energy that you, as an individualized energy, contemplate the need to experience this remembrance on a physical dimension (level).

The energy of your soul group holds or has the collective, overall remembrance of who you are and why you are. The energy understands, for it is intellect at its most rapid formation, which you came from. It is the GOD-Seed, that which you were (will evolve to) or more correctly, evolve at.

Now, when you evolve to (and hence move into) a physical form, you are still **a part of** the soul energy (soul group), yet you also have the energy of **apart from**. Not to be confused with separate to, although most people make that assumption.

It is the divinely inspired evolvement of the physical form to unify body, mind and soul. It brings into harmony the evolvement of your soul with the sustainable remembrance of the GOD-Seed intellect (or energy). The physical vibration has the energy of unified wholeness in a Vibrational Molecular Structure.

Once you as an individualized soul embark on the adventure of physical life, you are (so it seems), confronted with the daily dreariness of physical life.

As a child up to the age of 6 or 7, you have the full realization and remembrance of who you are and why you are. This is why stories of adventure are played out with feverish imagination. Through the gifts and creativity, our invisible friends dare us, laugh with us and share, learn and teach us everything we will need for future learning.

Once a child starts school, imagination is played down somewhat, due to the 'conforming' ideas of a child's collective growth. The individualized part of the soul learns to become more distanced or introspective.

Collective learning has taken over and left the individual learning behind. Once we, as a collective consciousness, but more as an individual consciousness, bring in or evolve to the energy of acceptance and remembrance, the molecular structure on a whole will become freer and less dense in energy.

The energy will then oscillate at a more rapid or accelerated rate of remembrance when we come together as a whole and it will work on the individualized remembrances to a fuller extent.

The remembrance and reconnection of the individualized soul group will reunite us all to our own destiny. Now we can all move into the full realization of who we are and why we are by contacting and becoming aware of our individualized soul energy or group. Remember, they are a part of you and not separate from you, therefore acknowledging the connection is relatively easy to do. Once you evolve yourself to an awareness of your soul's energy group around you, you will notice a feeling of exhilaration or awe move through you.
In allowing the energy its full movement, you will then begin to access your own information about your soul's destiny.

It may come in dream sequences, visions or déjà vu. In allowing yourself the energy of full realization, you will then begin, almost unknowingly, to live your destiny to its full extent.

By Universal law, as it stands collectively, only when you become aware or evolve to the full realization of your selfworth and remembrance on a whole can you then begin to access information or intellect on a more defined level. On this defined level, you accept not only who you are and why you are but also the acceptance of other souls who are closely connected to you (family, friends, loved ones and so on). Acceptance is allowing another soul to have their own destiny, individually as well as collectively. In remembering the GOD-Seed within all of us, we establish the truth as ALL is One, is One. We acknowledge another soul's right to choose.

This is one of the greatest gifts of remembrance that you could ever value and master. In this practice of nonjudgment and living with no-expectations, you witness the divine plan of yourself coming into full enlightenment and realization.

Accessing your own soul group energy then enables you to live as you were intended to live - in the moment - without fear and judgment, in pure love and peace-filled energy, always acknowledging the GOD-Seed within and the GOD without. You see and know that everything is **apart from you**, as it is **a part of you**.

Leaving Time Behind

In communicating with Jason on the subjects outlined in this book, I found that I personally had to become accustomed to the belief and energy of 'All is one, is One'.

As the conversations became more intense in their spiritual nature, I found that in speaking to Jay I firstly had to connect with the feeling and the thoughts that Jay is now part of everything. HE is everywhere. As is all energy. He is the wind blowing in the trees as well as the leaves being blown by that same wind.

I found it beneficial to connect with that particular energy of 'everything is everything'. When I did this, communication with Jay flowed freer and more fluently.

I was able then to call on his personality "as the" eternal energy, whereas in the first part of the book I could call him and he would "come through" the eternal energy.

I realized that in doing this I was able to again find a love for my brother that was stronger than I ever thought possible to feel for another human being.

This great love, this eternal love that Jason became, has enabled me to face a lot of fears and restrictions that I had place upon myself for a long time.

Eternal love and eternal energy is an awesome and intricately powerful thought/feeling structure that is so much a part of every single one of us.

The following conversations with Jay are on a more intense spiritual subject matter than the writings in the previous pages.

Jay speaks wonderfully about Angels and the intricate part they have played and continue to play in our lives.

He also explains about the GOD-seed soul that he has spoken of so often and its many healing and energy structures.

The only wish that Jay and I have is that those of you who read this book realize the great energy of choice and how it plays such a constant role in all our lives.

All is one, is One.

Nicole 2012

**Oh how I miss my Son! How proud I am of him and what he achieved and who he became. His capacity for love of all people was enormous
Journal Entry 27/1/99 Mum.**

Love = Evolve

If you look at numerology (another interesting science which delves into why we are and who we are), you will see that the E in our alphabet is a 5 - representing Freedom from your own limitations, and the V is a 22 - a Universal master number, (2 represents communication, compassion and unity).

So LOVE means - freedom from your own limitations, through communication, compassion and unity. EVOLVE - means freedom from your own limitations, through learning to utilize compassion and unity with love.

The collective memory is a fascinating subject to watch.

Through space and time (which of course was born out of collective memories), we can bear witness to the struggle that we have created to emphasize that evolvement through LOVE is the only answer we need. Time and time again, this is what is found to be the answer.

Back to the colors. As I said before, when you breathe in and out, the energy changes. Colors become more intricate and others more subtle. It's like a dance of light. Exactly like the wave of color energy in Alaska (Aurora). If you can remember the scene out of the movie "The Abyss", where the intellectual life form gently manipulates water through its own collective consciousness to portray a more human-like appearance, that's what energy does exactly.

It feels the collective consciousness awareness around and through itself and then changes (manipulates seems too harsh a word), according to those feelings or memories.

I tried to push at the colors because they seemed so solid, but instead of them moving away, the colors moved into my space or energy, even more. It was almost gel-like. It was (and is) amazing to play with. It uses our collective consciousness to enable itself to grow and evolve. At one point, when it moved around my hand, thousands of smiling faces formed through the colors. I can honestly say that it has become my friend and we learn a lot from each other.

I call it a friend because it is as much a part of me as it is apart from me. Energy is a highly intuitive intellect.

Try this visualization - Next time you have a bath, sit still and feel the energy of the water around you, not its wetness, but its energy. Lift yourself into a state of non-judgment (in that way you don't expect anything), and then turn to a mirror that you have positioned next to you. Politely ask the energy to come and play. You'll be fascinated with what you see. Your appearance will completely change. And in that change of appearance, you will begin to grasp an insight into what I now call my world, my playground. There is so much to learn here - so many questions answered, so many memories coming back to me.

The expansion of the mind is an amazingly wonderful thing. You can grasp hold of intellect (its real - you can touch it!), and ask it to allow its collective memory to become one with yours. It already is of course, you just have to remember that fact - and that's all the part of the fun and learning.

There's so much to share with you about what I am experiencing and remembering. I have to remember that Earth's energy is a lot denser than the energy where I am in, only because Earth herself has forgotten. I love you. Your dreams are reality.

Remember them.

How you EVER gonna know

Listen not to the critics
Who put their own Dreams on the shelf
If you want to get the truth to admit it
you gotta find out for yourself

Anything in Life worth having
Lord, it has its sacrifice
But the gift that you're receiving
Is worth more than the price

There ain't nobody in this world
that's gonna do it for you

Do what you gotta do

— Jesus 1998 —

The ART of Purpose

PURPOSE / per-puhs / - n. - Intention to act. 2. resolution, determination.

To live with purpose or purposely is why we are here. To have the full intention of purposeful living, focused in mind as well as the body, to strive, search, grow and learn with intention, with purpose.

Many of us have no idea what it is to be intentional let alone to live with the intention of purpose; but through the many years since my brother Jay, Passed through Time, he has spoken strongly of purposeful living.

Acknowledging the self-confidence and recognizing the purpose of our own individual life, is hard to comprehend but so easy to obtain.

Jay, what is living purposely? If life is all pre-destined hasn't the purpose been shown already and we are just going through the motions?

No. Not at all. I have found and learnt from many situations from Passing through Time where human beings have no purpose to living or more importantly haven't found a purpose to their own life.

Human beings are conditioned from birth to strive, learn and grow, but only to the society's idealism of that life. So many times in my own life I forgot to act with the purpose of living, instead acting 'on' or 'to' the purpose. I have found in many areas of life; in other forms as well as our own, that few of us have actually learnt or sub-consciously live with the intention of purpose.

Purpose is a fragmented energy identified with other forms of energy as in love, hope and optimism as these energies correlate and expand in their own energy-based form, the energy is heightened by movement of the energy that is 'within' your body and that which passes 'through' your body.

Purpose is an intention; there is no separating the two energies. Living 'with' purpose will allow your life to bring into itself an awesome energy that corresponds with the energies of success, fruition and completion.

So many of us strive for something tangible to hold onto through life, whether that comes into a form of faith, acceptance, the love of another etc. But I have seen purpose in action and it's incredible to witness. When you see something or someone who has struggled throughout life, then through the art of purpose, their life changes to that of positivity and gratefulness of all things all lessons, no longer seeing life as a burden but a blessing and then living that - I'm telling you it's mind blowing.

Jay, what color is purpose? Does it even have a purpose?
The color energy of purpose is that of a deep purple.

Purpose or the energy of purpose correlates with that of both right and left brain affecting all neurons (nerve-cells). The energy of purpose stimulates both sides of the brain so that there is no misjudgment or misalignment of thought patterns with the intent of purpose. Because of this strong energy-based form it conducts the behavioral as well as the creative sides of the human form.

Once living in the energy of purpose with intent, the color rapidly changes into sharp bursts of Vibrant Electric Blue. When I saw this happening to someone, I noticed that the whole body of the person had changed.

Where once they slouched or never looked anyone in the eyes for fear of ridicule or shame dwelling, they now stood with strength, their mannerisms changed from pessimistic to optimistic and through their eyes - you could see focus.

Jay, how can we all live with purpose?

Make the choice.
It's that simple.
Choose to live with purpose. Focus on your purpose. Purpose has millions of energy fragmentations, so that allows an infinite number of choices.

1 *Choose* to be the best person you can be and live that purpose.
2 *Choose* to be kind to yourself and live that purposely.
3 *Choose* to be loved and love and live that purposely.
4 *Choose* to be free, choose to be happy.
5 *Choose* to see every lesson in life as a miracle and every miracle a blessing and when you do that, when you do all these things, purposely with true intention, that's when you become great.

That's when you become Immortal.

Purpose flows into every single lesson in life. All it depends on is you. You can choose to use purpose diligently, allowing the energy to correspond with your entire being. You can choose to act with purpose when your energy escalates to a point of...

The Purpose of Intentional Happiness.

Happiness is an internal energy structure that not only works on the body's well-being and overall optimistic outlook on life, but also works with the adrenals, stimulating and producing endorphins from the brain. This allows the body to live within the energy of free expression.

To fully experience and appreciate true happiness we must first let go of any expectations and judgments that we have held onto throughout our lives but also those thoughts that we have and are working through internally. Focusing on the energy of purposeful happiness, allow yourself to 'feel' to the full extent how joyous life is. You will be rewarded in so many ways. Blessings unfold. Miracles happen. Remember always, what you focus on you receive.

Letting go of the restrictions that you have chosen for your own life will enable you to move through to energy of unlimited potential. No longer doubting the internal happiness and joy, your body begins to resonate with that energy as you 'become' that energy.

Be mindful of your thoughts. Choose a positive outlook. Do not become 'happier' but choose to be happy. There is a huge difference in those two words. Becoming and choosing. When you strive to 'become' you continue to focus more on the energy of that which you don't have.

When you choose, you have already made the decision. Your body is instantly transformed into a powerful, positive spiritual being because you are focusing on what you are, not what you may become.

Remember choice.

Continuing to move through (not into but through), the intention of happiness your life will focus on positive uplifting sequences and events in your life.

Jay, I have a friend who is perpetually in happiness. Every time you see her she is warm, sincere, focused and happy.
When I once asked how she got to be so happy, what was her secret, she said "so many of us focus on a negative mind frame, you know, bills due this week, kids need to be fed, work driving them crazy, partner not 'there' for them anymore blah, blah, blah. I looked around at my friends, family and work colleagues one day and didn't like what I saw.
My whole life existed in a negative mindset. So I chose different.
You'd be amazed at how easy it is, and also how many people feel threatened by it. They are so 'caught' in their intention to disagree, to negate, and to manifest such absurd loneliness and isolation. They can't see the trees from the weeds. So now when people ask me how my day is, I say Great! Even when it seems everything is becoming on top of me, I focus on a positive intention.
I'd rather not see the cup half full OR half empty. The way I see it is 'you have a choice to change things, so already you have a blessing'.

Focusing on what you have in your life and not what you are receiving is the key to perpetual happiness. Allowing yourself to be happy is sometimes hard for some people. The human experience seems to take over from the feelings of happiness. We only seem to notice our feelings when they override all other emotions.

Some days you don't feel like you are feeling any emotion whatsoever. How many of us at one point in our lives or another have ever been so consumed with a sickness - sometimes as simple as a head cold - and think to yourself - 'I don't remember how I felt when I was well'. Sometimes we are so consumed by what is happening to us right then and there that we forget to step back and look at the big picture. Focus on the now, live in the now, yes, but do not limit yourself by thinking this is the only thing that is happening to me'. Step back. Breathe. Then re-evaluate your emotional status.

Even in dire circumstances of severe depression, grief or sadness you can step back from the emotion and find yourself in an energy of happiness. So many times we wait for the huge emotion, the big re-evaluation of feelings and emotions, your energy whispers and gently guides us to the place we need to be. Be happy. Focus on your soul energy, allow yourself to be guided to the place of happiness. Allow yourself to feel. Do not limit yourself in accepting anything less than happiness.

What you become, you have lived. Memories help us recreate the experience of happiness. In our immortality we are able to perceive and accept emotions that have happened and are yet to happen. No longer focusing on the energies of fearfulness, guilt, shame, resentment, we can continue to move through life with happiness. Laughter is the only true human experience that is spontaneous. Laughter is the energy of happiness in its purest form. The energy of happiness fills your entire being until it quite literally bubbles over and becomes an 'experience' of happiness. Laugh. A lot! Laugh yourself stupid.
Laughter is infectious and never causes anyone sadness. Laugh at life. Laugh in the face of death.

Happiness can be reached simply by reacting in a positive mindset rather than continuing to flow through life negatively. Happiness is not a 'hippy' word. Happiness is your birthright.
Rightful living in all its glory becomes an area of life that we all need to concentrate on and become disciplined with. In the act of rightful living we become accustomed to honoring ourselves and living our live to the best of our ability. It allows us to move forward with the full knowledge of who we are and in this knowledge we see and know our ultimate choices in completing our personal destinies.

To come into the living of rightfulness we must first acknowledge our individual honoring - that which we hold dear, that which we accept with faith and hold tightly with love. In acknowledging those things we sacrifice all else for, we then prove to ourselves that we are indeed unique, powerful and universal. Nothing will stop us in the quest of rightful living. This is an honoring of all life throughout the ages, that which was once before us and that which is ahead of us. But to accomplish this energy configuration within us is the divine sacrifice.

We give up all things which do not reflect who we are as an individual and also collectively as a nation. For there is truly only one nation and that is the nation of life. The nation of living, of honor, discipline, love and faith. If we can only hold onto these few ideals of who we are, what makes us, what we stand by, then we will return to the ultimate quest, and then we will fulfill our destiny.

Without this search we will all continue to wander aimlessly throughout time, only picking up fragments, small pieces that make up the whole. We will continue to suffer in silence, we will continue to fall apart.

Rightful living is a choice that is made individually. Know your place in the world then challenge that. Never succumb to second best. We are perfect beings, beings of amazing intellect. Beings who can love so deeply. Yet we have bowed to the thoughts and judgments of another's opinion.
No more. Challenge yourself. Every day, every waking minute ask yourself what you believe in, who you believe in. Strive, search and grow. It all happens simultaneously, but focus on that. Never lose sight of who you are. Become powerful, not power filled. Be humble. Live rightfully, purposefully, intentionally and live humbly.

Acknowledge the gift that lives inside of you. Shaping and evolving, searching, conquering fears and thoughts every minute of your life. Feel your power and in that power see how fragile you are. Not weak, but fragile. Fragility allows the human intellect to accept all life, all things as they are, no longer disturbing or breaking down the natural order of events, but moving, flowing with and evolving to be that which it observes.

In the honoring of yourself you become one with the ultimate intellect - that which is GOD - the Unified Consciousness. Honor is righteous. When we no longer push the destiny trail but ride along with it we find ourselves in magical places, witnessing miracles. Life surprises us constantly. Just when you think you have seen everything wonderful, that wonderment expands and grows ten-fold then one- hundred-fold 'till your heart bursts with love.

In honoring yourself, you honor all life, all things.

Love yourself. Learn to know yourself. Really learn to know yourself. Question everything - not with cynicism but with wonderment. Begin to ask how, not why. Feel every emotion to its full extent. Feel everything to its full extent. Feelings come from the truest source of intellect, pure feelings. Honor feelings. Honor another's. Honor all life, all things. Become happy. Contemplate GOD and smile when you do.

The ART of Loving Purposefully

Loving is the ultimate experience. Being loved, loving someone or something allows us to look deep within ourselves and become that which we are. In loving, the energy that surrounds us spikes and becomes turbulent, feverish and strong with the high fragmented energy of purpose.

Loving purposefully starts and ends with yourself. It is the wonderful energy of loving that allows us to find who we are constantly on a daily basis. Being 'in love' or in the loving energy of purposeful love, the emotions become so fragile, yet powerful that we begin to dream. Our dreams become awakened by this immense energy because we feel. Plain and simple. We have begun to feel and it feels great, so good that we want to continue to live in that energy of loving permanently. So we begin to search for things that will match that energy and once found, the energy of loving becomes so heightened, so extremely powerful that we feel we can do anything, and rightly so.
Because once tapped into, the energy of loving purposefully soars us to great heights and new wonderful dimensions.
In acknowledging the love we have for ourselves, life becomes so enriched with powerful messages and awesome blessings, because of course, like attracts like. In loving we are loved. That is a Universal Law.

IN LOVING WE ARE LOVED

In loving ourselves, we return the love that we are constantly sending away from ourselves, and in doing so, we acknowledge the divine within.

Finally coming into the realization that loving yourself is all you need, because once in that energy, the energy of giving love to yourself, you cannot help but be loving to all who surround you. Like attracts like.

In the energy of receiving love from yourself, your energy transforms and evolves into a perpetual state of bliss. No longer needing to find love outside yourself, no longer wanting someone to love you, to place their love onto you to make you feel loved, you find yourself in a more divine place in life. The divinity of love perpetuates and evolves into an infinite number of energy choices and lessons. The ultimate retrieval of the God-Self within is the loving you give to yourself.

Love yourself. Your mind, body, thoughts. Love who you are and who you are becoming. Love your soul. Love yourself as you love GOD, for you are one and the same.

You are not separate. You are not alone. You are loved. In loving, we are loved.

Change your Thoughts – Change your Life.

I want to tell you about what I have learnt and remembered about the choices we make. From day to day, minute to minute, the life we make is a choice - our choice.

Choice is our own personal experience that no unseen force can alter or stop in any way. By unseen force I mean no outside influence, be it other persons, situations, entities etc,.
Now, from what I've witnessed since passing, everything is a choice - everything. From the experiences you have, to the people you connect or don't connect with, right down to the color of your underwear you are wearing right now, it is all a choice.

The most interesting thing about choice and thought is that it is all predestined. Every single choice you make has already been chosen. You've already lived through it. You planned it, lived through it and now remember the choices you made and most importantly, what you learnt while living through the experience of your choices. Your own individual choices are your own. Collective consciousness is also a choice. You can either be part of the crowd and think as others do or stand aside and choose to think, feel and act differently. It's up to you, it is your choice. You've already experienced absolutely everything that you're ever going to do, think, feel and act.

That's the amazing thing about life.
It's already been.

Try not to over-think or pre-judge the event or outcome because of course, there is a million to one chance that you will not go through the outcome you are dreading or terrified of going through. And if by chance (or choice), you do go through exactly what you visualized - I'm talking about the negative aspects we may think and feel at times the only thing you need to do is realize you have already done it, even the other million choices (chances).

I'll give you a scenario which is based on fact - it just hasn't fully been realized yet.

You start work at eight in the morning.
1. You get up before the alarm goes off, - or
2. The alarm wakes you, - or
3. You sleep right through till 11:30 a.m.

1. Because you got up early, you decided to file some mail and realized that you forgot to pay the phone company.

2. The alarm wakes you, you shower, shave, dress and head for work.

3. You turn over and in a sleep-filled daze look at the clock and realizing the time, you jump out of bed, accidentally kick the cat and stub your toe.

4. You turn over and in a sleep-filled daze, look at the clock, notice the time, reach for the phone and call work and tell them that you're not coming in.

All of those scenarios happen. Every single one, plus a million more. If you still have trouble re-membering, or believing that this is the way life truly is - then watch the TV show 'Sliders' and movies 'Sliding Doors' and 'Groundhog day'.

It's all going to happen, because it has already happened. There is no choice about it: That's the choice. You can go along merrily and feel you have one life to live and you're going to do your best at it (which is the most evolving way to live) and that's your choice.

You can believe, choose to believe and live knowing that you have bad karma stored from hundreds of years back and your life is going to be shit till you pay your universal debts and that's the way you will live, that's your choice You can live your life knowing that you are born from sin and there's nothing that you can do about it and hope on your judgment day that God's in a good mood or you're going straight to a big burning furnace in the ground called 'hell', (which by the way doesn't exist - which is what I choose to believe), that's your choice.

Everything is choice, everything is chosen ... Therefore, the one thing I have learnt - the only thing that needs to be learnt - is to love yourself, as you are divine, beautiful and holy. See others as divine, beautiful and holy. Live your talk, walk your walk, laugh a lot, have fun and remember nothing is too serious that hasn't been got through.

I love you. Jason

Jay, could you explain to me further about choice please. I still do not understand why someone would choose to be raped, murdered or in a serious car accident?

Remember, they are very extreme cases you are speaking of. Let me put it this way: Choice is chance. For example, the explanation of disease, where a disease will find and gravitate/oscillate at its own Vibrational Molecular Structure, so too does choice. Choice is energy in an extreme form.
I say extreme, because it is an intricate part of all life. When thought/feeling vibration molecules are accelerated through, in and around the human body, they will naturally occur in, or oscillate with, the energy that is conclusive with their own.
Water finds its own level.
Energy corresponds with exactly the same energy as itself.

Therefore, your choices gravitate and oscillate with you, because that is what you are oscillating and vibrating at, right at that moment.

When you begin to grow mentally, spiritually and emotionally and begin to make more self-aware choices, then the choices you make become more defined. You become aware of choice when you become evolved with your own personal Vibrational Molecular Structure.

Life choice (I feel the word 'karma' has been tainted so I'll use the words 'life choice'), is highlighted by your life review before birth. These lessons or chances at accelerated learning for you as a human being, are brought to you, by you, to enable you to become a better or more "evolved" human being. They allow you major shifts of energy, enabling growth and the enlightenment of your Self, to yourself.

So, in the body's capacity to align itself with healthy molecules or dis-eased molecules, so it is with 'life choices'. The only way to change your life is by choosing different and vibrating at that different level.

Jay, I still don't understand about choice. I don't understand why someone would chose to be raped, molested or just have nothing good ever happen to them?

Remember, your individualized divine plan is a part of your intellect. It is the energy that 'drives' you. In the instance of being raped or molested, it is a contractual agreement between both people (read 'Little Soul and The Sun' by Neale Donald Walsch). The energy that you create out of your thoughts and feelings is what the intellect then perceives or forms into a real situation.
Remember - like attracts like. Never think that you sit there and think: "I'm going to have a car accident today, just because I want to". That is not how it works. You vibrate at an individual molecular structure and a collective molecular structure.

Jay, why do I still fear confrontation so much after all my learning and remembering of choice?

You still 'see' around you that people are un-evolved in the aspects of the divine life that they can live and this ultimately threatens your very existence. The old 'new age' saying that 'everyone is a mirror of yourself', becomes less of an insight and more of a self-fulfilled prophecy.
You tend to bring to you, around you, those people who will allow you to believe that humans just haven't 'got it' yet.

The full knowledge of who you are and why you are begins to waiver as you become entwined with their restrictions and judgments of your life.
Remember this - judgment, or to judge, is to break down the very existence of the divine intellect into categories or boxes. You then become separated and dissected until unrecognizable to your own self as 'divine'.

Why do I still put myself in those situations? I still feel the fight or flight energy well up inside me.

Remember this - people are scared. Fear is welling up inside of them so rapidly that it is choking their very remembrance of the divine.
The GOD-Seed is unrecognizable in themselves because they are still evolving at the Vibrational Molecular Structure of 'all for one'. They have not yet remembered the joy of least resistance.
The new Millennium came towards them so rapidly that they have no other instinct, but to lash out. This is the only way they can feel power-filled and less dominated by those people and those situations they have chosen to create around them. It is their survival instinct. It is the only way they know.

How can we help them remember?

You can't. Every single person has the right to choose their life and the way they live it. You can only raise your own energy through remembrance of who you are and why you are. In that remembrance, you evolve at a more rapid Vibrational Molecular Structure that will have an effect on how you live your own life.

Remember, like dis-ease not being able to manifest in a body that is not evolving at its own personal Vibrational Molecular Structure so too certain experiences cannot manifest in your life when you are evolving at a different Vibrational Molecular Structure.

The beings that are evolving at the same Vibrational Molecular Structure will naturally gravitate to and affect those at the same level as themselves.

Likewise, the beings that evolve at a more rapid Vibrational Molecular Structure gravitate to and affect those who are at the same evolvement as themselves.

Talk later. Breathe and extend yourself.

Well today kind of sucked and I'm so grateful for that. Just makes me realize more and more that I don't was going to say 'belong'- grow spiritually, emotionally or physically there (at work). I know the wheels are turning and I'm moving into a faster vibration where more and more positive situations are being drawn to me - but I feel like I consciously 'lower' my energy when I'm there just so I can fit in with everyone else.

I did my 5 positive powerful high rapid vibrational words till I was almost screaming them out physically. Instead I just screamed them in my head.

Why do I feel I need to fit in?
Why do I have such a negative belief system such as 'people aren't talking to me which means I have done something wrong?'
How can I get out of this 'it's all about me' energy?

I'm going to take back what I said at the beginning of this question. I do and am growing spiritually, emotionally and physically there, I truly just don't 'belong' there.

Bravo Nicole. That's exactly right. You picked up on the energy today that was the denser energy.. And even thou you felt 'out of place', you still never gave up with your high rapid vibrational thoughts. I'm so proud of you. And you learned such a valuable lesson about energy today. About how it feels to not only live in high vibrational energy, but also how to act within it. You continued to be open and honest even when you felt 'weird'.
Remember we spoke about energy matching energy? What did you truly feel to your core today?

That I wanted to get away from there as quickly as I could.
That's because you felt the pull of the Universe. The energy moving around you was propelling you forward. You may not have felt that was the case, but that's exactly what was happening. Now, there are two things you can do when you're in that particular vibration.

One is quite simply grin and bear it 'till it's over or, and this is most important, you can focus on more and more positive thoughts and visualizations, drawing to you more vibrational energy that will be moving you closer and closer towards where you truly 'fit' in.

Even today when surrounded by boxes and concrete you could have externally focused on beautiful things - the smile on a friend's face, then sound of laughter or stepped outside briefly and focused on the sky, the way the trees swayed gently in the breeze.

Breathe that scene in, drawn it inside of you till you knew that the sky is part of you, that the tree is part of you, that you are not, and have never been separate from it.

You're toying with the idea of fewer hours there. Why could that be a bad thing? Especially when you feel you don't belong. You see the things is, you are working more and more hours on your writing, not just with me but you're other novels and screenplays. Don't you see that you are moving into the energy of 'full time writer?' 1 day less at work, means 1 day more where you can write, means more positive energy in your life, for yourself.

More knowledge shared, more and more vibrational energy accumulating and expanding outwardly from you, drawing you closer and closer to more positive uplifting insights and adventures.

Do it because you know it's right. And the money is going to flow like a raging river when you do.
You fear ridicule, you fear isolation, and you fear being ostracized by your peers. Yet you live in freedom. Find truth in being free and continue to push the boundaries of society's concept of life and how to live it. Your feelings of fear are only your lack of faith. Lack of belief in yourself. Let's look at the words ridicule, isolation and ostracized. These are words that describe a person feeling totally alone with completely no support network doesn't it? You are never NEVER alone Nicole. You, of all people, should know that. In your darkest hour I will light your way. You are never without my guidance, my love and my understanding.

But have the faith and belief in yourself that you light your own way. You Nicole, light your path. It is your strength, your spirit and your soul that guide you. Do you truly believe you hate yourself that much too ever put yourself in harm's way? In a situation you couldn't turn and walk away from? You Scorpio's are so dramatic at times. (Laughs)

Remind yourself that life isn't at all supposed to be this hard and truly not this serious. Laugh out loud when you hear that inner dialogue tell you that you're not worth it, that everyone is angry with you. Tell it, it needs to come up with something a hell of a lot better than that to get you to lower your energy. Sing. Laugh. Dance. Move rapidly when your denser dialogue rears its ugly head.

And Nicole, why you're feeling like it is always all about you, is because it IS all about you. This is your life. If it weren't all about you, you'd be straight back at the beginning of this chapter again.

Because if it's not 'all about you' it's 'all about everyone else'. Welcome to becoming selfish. (laughs) Soon it will become fun again I promise.

As a collective consciousness, today is the day of your remembrances and your resurgence into the human race. The ultimate test of faith is that of the strongest will and remembrance of your divine plan - collectively and individually.

Through grieving we find love and through love we find, or more importantly, remember who were are and why we are.

Remember, grieving takes many forms.

Humans, as emotional beings, try to forget their weaknesses instead of embracing them. Yet, it is by embracing weakness that makes the human 'be-ing' stronger. Until we know what can break us and what makes us vulnerable, we fear everything. Once knowledge of our own personal as well as collective fear or vulnerability is reached, we can move forward in the knowledge that nothing can harm us, emotionally as well as physically, unless we choose that experience.

Once knowledge of such a lesson is reached, we strive forward with the confidence of who we are and why we are, knowing there is not one thing that we cannot learn from, grow, teach others and most importantly move on from. The most important realization after that knowledge is reached, is the energy of letting go. Letting go of the energy of mistakes, personal judgments as well as collective judgments, brings the human race into a more rapid alignment with its individualized association with the GOD-Seed, which is in all of us.

Once that remembrance of the non-judgment lifestyle that we are all sanctioned by is reached, our collective and individualized Vibrational Molecular Structure evolves at a more rapid energy.

Jay, I understand about living in non-judgment, but what about judgment of life? When you passed did you receive any judgment, or did you witness a 'life review' (as some people call it?)

There is no such thing as the energy of judgment where I am. Once you have passed and greeted and embraced all who you think and feel, you do witness a review or revision of your life, showing you how you progressed and learned your planned lessons.

It's like an overview of everything you have said and done, but more importantly, everything you have thought and felt. You look upon this revision or review with the energy of completion.

Before you are born into a physical body, you review your coming life in intricate detail. You choose which parents, country, race and economic structure that will most benefit you and help you to remember an aspect of the 'who you are and why you are' in that particular vibrational molecular experience.
As I said before, at birth or (more importantly) at conception, you review the experiences of the life you have chosen.

This life will be lived to benefit you greatly. It will help you to recognize and demonstrate to yourself who you are and why you are, to the best of your ability through the lessons and choices that you make.

You not only 'see' your own individual vibrational molecular destiny, but you also 'see' how your individual destiny grows and correlates with the destiny of human collective consciousness and Universal consciousness.
So you are indeed a unique and valuable part of the Earth's collective consciousness and ultimate destiny. Without your personal insights, choices, lessons and experiences, the web could not be completed.
At the end of your life, after Passing through Time, you then review how your life progressed and 'weaved' itself through that particular Vibrational Molecular Structure. It is as if you were a long-jumper looking back on your efforts, but without criticisms or judgments.

You can then choose your next experience. This could be in the form of another 'life' on Earth, where you reexperience the choices you made. Here you learn and grow in your life's lessons, watching for the signs of coincidences, chance meetings and opportunities for the valuable growth of your life's lessons.

Is that what déjà vu is - coincidences and chance meetings?

Déjà vu is an intricate energy of remembrances, similar to that of a child leaving cookie crumbs on their path of adventure.
This amazing energy of remembrance helps us spiritually and intellectually to know or recall that we have indeed been here before, doing this very thing that we are experiencing.
It is a personal clue that you have given yourself before birth, to allow yourself the gift of recognizing that you are on the 'right path'.

Apart from returning to a new 'lifetime', there are an infinite number of other choices you can make after Passing through Time. These include returning to the God-Source (the ultimate experience for a soul), learning from other beings of intellect and remembrances and/or choosing (as I have done), to reunite with the all-knowing through memories and remembrances. By doing this, I am able to communicate with you through my and your feelings so that others may know and remember the true adventure of "Soul Searching".

Remember, there are infinite choices you can make here and all of them happen simultaneously. As here on Earth, in Heaven. As in life, in death.

So to answer your question - No, there are no judgments or critical remarks from a 'higher' authority. You are your own judge, for who can judge you more harshly that yourself? (I am using the words 'judgment' and 'judging' here because there are no human words to explain where I resonate). You are in a space of all knowing, all loving, pure peace-filled energy. The only words that I can explain that might help you understand are these: When you are viewing your life, you are unattached to what is **going** to **happen** and then what has happened.
All is One, is One.
I love you, and am with you all.
There is nothing to fear.
All is as it should be.

Jay, why? Why do we - as a collective consciousness as well as an individualized consciousness - accept the failures and fears more than the best that life has to offer us?

Firstly, you already answered that with your question. You state that you *accept* fear, failure etc. before or more importantly, ahead of laughter, joy, hope and love because you see that life - not your true self - offers it to you. You accept your fears and failures. That's what you see in your life.
But, you feel you are only *offered* love, joy and hope. You are still in the Vibrational Molecular Structure of 'I am not worthy'. Do you understand?

I think so.

Let me put it this way, elaborating more on the human phenomenon of self-worth, or lack thereof.

Humans have the tendency to put a price on everything. Not just things house, car, boat etc, but everything including **self-joy**, **self-hope** and **self-love**.

I'll start with the latter first - Self Love.

Self - Love

Self-Love is what we are - Plain and simple. We are created out of the 'divine' Vibrational Molecular Structure of love of self, to strive and grow through love so we may evolve into love, becoming a part of and not apart from love.

To achieve this self-love, we need to remember to delve deep in our memories to find the space where we first experienced love within, as well as outside of ourselves. It may have been love for a parent, friend, and a pet or in later years, a lover or a partner.

Now, in finding that core, that particular memory, step back and acknowledge how you felt before you experienced love outside of yourself. Was there a feeling of fear, self-loathing, or of joy and happiness?

Remember the scene perfectly in your mind, access your intellect. Allow the memory to shine through like sunlight.
Breathe - not deeply or shallowly, just breathe. Fill your mind with memories. Now access the memory. Feel the space around you. How does it feel? Is it comfortable, confronting, or accepting? Remember, none of your feelings are wrong or right:

They are just feelings. There is no judgment here.
Remember the smells, listen to the sounds. Are they familiar or unfamiliar? Does your breathing remain calm, relaxed or anxious, hesitant? Allow those feelings to come.

This is your intellect's way of helping you to remember.

It is still living in that space. Remember, you have chosen this time to find your self-love, to return it to yourself. You are strong, protected and you are not alone. Now, breathe in the memory of that instant when self-love became a separate reality. How does it feel? Is it gently flowing from you to another? Or does it feel shocking, abusive, and confrontational?

Allow the tears to come. They are a cleansing and your intellect's way of showing you that you just love deeply and that you are willing to acknowledge the wound and heal it through remembrance of you, the divine.

Now, put your hands on the place where your body is aching. The memory has been living, manifested in your body through your thoughts and actions of self-protection. Your body is your safeguard. Does your body, weep, scream in silence, or feel comfort at the knowledge of remembrance? Allow all feelings to come. Remember, it is through choice that you experience those memories.

It is now your choice to let the memories go and return the love back to yourself. Sit still in that space for a while, as the memories resurface.

Imagine now a light mist falling above, around and through you. Lift your arms up and acknowledge the multitude of colors swirling and dancing around you.
Which color is the strongest? Which is the lightest?
Breathe in the mist and as you do so, see the colors filling your very being, inside and around your body. Feel 'part of' everything.

Allow yourself the gift of this visualization once a week until you acknowledge that you live the visualization. Be reassured in the knowledge that you are taking nothing away from anyone or anything.

It is apart from you and a part of you. Self-Love is like breathing. It never ends. The only reason you feel lost from it is because you feel it is something that you make happen or is offered to you.

Love is all you are - energy evolved in a Vibrational Molecular Structure that allows feelings to materialize and form into itself and apart from itself. You are a divine intellect that acknowledges that there is something more, yet nothing outside of itself. Now, self-hope.

Self – Hope

Hope is the energy of the soul that is the reassurance of the divine plan, including but not excluding, your individualized divine plan. Hope is the energy of anticipation, the allknowing. It is the energy of miracles and coincidences. It is always with us, inside of us, a part of us.

Hope allows us to remember to strive for more evolving thoughts and feelings. Hope manifests in self-love.
Similar to the energy of self-deprecation, the feeling of losing self-hope is a slow process. The energy of self-hope seems diminished by the feelings of lack, resistance and the acknowledgement of conforming idealism. Self-hope is resisted by those who live in the energy of sadness, plain and simple - sadness for themselves, but also and most alarmingly, sadness for the material, economical and spiritual energy of the planet.
They have forgotten their true right of freedom - freedom to love, to wish and to dream. They have lost or given up their right to remember the divine plan.

Their own individual divine plan has become squashed and depleted with the energy of self-loathing, unworthiness, cynicism and fear.

They have truly 'lost' their way. They have abandoned their excitement for the gift of a miraculous life, so therefore in seeing no 'hope' for themselves, they manifest energy into that 'hopeless' vibration.

All that they touch and see is crumbling, taken from them before their eyes.

They feel there is nothing more that can be one. Time has run out. So, more and more, they create the energy of hopelessness around them creating exactly what they choose to feel and think.

If you feel you are in this space, **try this visualization.**

Imagine yourself in a field.
What does the field feel like? Is it lush and green, with a stream nearby, or is it barren and downtrodden from years of resistance? Remember, no feeling is wrong or right - Just feelings. There is no judgment here.

Now, feel the wind lightly touch your face. You cannot see wind, but you know it IS. It is there to remind you of the miracle of hope. The wind is teaching you a strong remembrance. It is allowing you to recognize that nothing is unreal, everything is possible.

See that the wind, although not seen with the eyes, touches things, changing their stance, allowing them to remember the freedom of movement.

Notice if the wind blows hard across your face or lightly caresses you. Do you feel yourself resist its dance or became drawn to join in?
Allow the feeling of your body's movement. Breathe naturally. Feel your body come alive with the anticipation of miraculous movement.
Notice a tree in front of you. Is it swaying with the dance of the wind, or bending and distorting with every breath? How does the tree 'feel'?

Breathe in the visualization for a long time. Find yourself become one with the gentleness of the wind.
Allow yourself to move with the tree's movements.
Mirror the tree's movements.
Now, allow yourself to 'look' closely at the tree. Are there many leaves? Is it a huge Oak, or a small sapling? Is it gnarled with age and resistance, or flourishing and bright with flexibility?

Acknowledge the scars of the tree. See, with the growth rings of the tree, that it is apart from you as much as it is a part of you. The tree has grown as you have. There are emotional scars on its body, just as you have.

Count how many branches are on your tree. Notice how more branches appear as you let go of resistance and welcome the change of its movement and its structure.

Feel the tree move into your own being, its energy growing excitedly inside of you - stretching, reaching for new experiences, new movements that will allow it to grow, to learn, to live in the divine splendor of its miraculous structure.

Now, see yourself flourish with new ideas, growing in excitement and anticipation of your new insight of your own divine plan. Stretch, reaching forward and upward, toward the sunlight and the remembrance of who you are and why you are.
Walk each day with the knowledge of this new resurgence of energy, in tune with your own divine being. Become accustomed to searching new avenues, never fearing the outcome, knowing that every experience is a growing and learning of your remembrance.
Now, self-joy.

Self-Joy

Even when Self-Joy is felt, it brings the energy of wonderment and laughter. Self-Joy is a realization of who you are and why you are.
It is the ultimate realization of choice. Self-Joy is the inevitable outcome of choosing to evolve with self-love and self-hope. In joy, there is no judgment.
Joy is expressed with the full knowledge of the divine within all of us and within every single thing. It cannot be escaped from because it is an intricate part of who you are and why you are. It allows us to live in our truth.
Joy enables us the right to choose for the betterment of our highest selves. Its energy evolves at a rapid vibrational molecular level which casts away self-doubt and the energy of being miserable.
Joy allows us to become the energy that we really are - joyous Beings, evolving and learning with the intellect of miraculous energy.

Now, try this visualization.

Feel the energy of yourself in your field. Notice the greenness and lushness of the grass. See that your tree has become strong and beautiful in the realization of all that it has become.

Notice a stream to your left. Is it flowing gently between the rocks, is it rushing with feverish force, or is it stagnant and surrounded by a dry, parched river bed?

Remember, no feelings are wrong or right - just feelings. There is a no judgment here.
Feel the water as it makes its way past the river banks.

Notice if any moss is clouding the water. Are there logs obstructing the flow of the water?
Allow yourself to feel the destiny of the water as it flows and searches, learns and teaches, giving life to all who come across it. Breathe in the energy of that destiny.
Choose to see the river connected to the ocean. Choose to feel its individual path, once small, then many, now one with its ultimate source.

Feel in your own life your destiny's path. See that you were once also regarded as 'small'. Then acknowledge your learning and growth has become many parts of yourself. You now touch and inspire all you meet, as they look upon the miracle that is you - the divine you.
Feel the choice in your path. Become one with the excitement that is building inside your very being, the essence of who you are and why you are.

Allow yourself to remember that all is as it should be.

Feel the joyous celebration of choice blow through your life, creating, changing, and evolving what you choose to experience.

This vital busy young man - gone for us - but busy, vital and happy where he is now, greeting souls, nurturing and caring.
Now, Pure Love, Pure Light.
Journal Entry - 27/1/99 Mum

Do Angels Exist?

Jay, are there actually Angels among us?

I take great pride in saying that the Angels are amongst my closest friends. They have taught me how to remember the divine spark of wisdom in all of us.

Angels are part of the Vibrational Molecular Structure of the Universe. They play an intricate part in not only human memories and 'miracles', but also other worlds - as they themselves come from another world - separate to, but a part of Earth's vibrational molecular destiny.

Angels were born out of Intellect/Energy's great wisdom and wonderment of all things pure and innocent. With the word innocent, please do not confuse this with naiveté. For they are anything but naive. The Angels' humor amazes me. Their practical sense of realism and fantasy astounds me, and their unconditional Love they show to all beings inspires me to greater heights of love than I have ever felt, or felt capable of.

They are mysterious and adventurous. They have taken me under their wings (no pun intended), and shown me such fascinating insights into not only human intellect and evolvement, but their own and others as well.

They are indeed among us. Humans have this absurd perception that the Angels are here just for humankind. But certainly this is not the case. They are the helpers, and those who remember all life, all energy. They are the harbingers of good news, joyous events and pure Love.

Throughout Earth's early history, they did indeed walk and play among the people, animals and plant life. Their soul purpose is to manifest energy to a greater - not better - but greater energy, when judgment of life or the Divine Plan is mislaid. They are here to help us as human 'beings' to remember the miracle of the divine plan.

The spontaneous vibrational energy that flows through these beings is an amazing sight to witness. Angels shower unlimited amounts of grace and empowerment to humankind, as to all of life.

Mikail, or Archangel Michael as he is commonly known on Earth, is a total practical joker. He is built solid, with an immense amount of energy that pulses highly (like a sonar), when he concentrates on miraculous events, such as the birth of a child, an infant calf's first steps, or a home run out of left field.

No event is more important than any other, because that would then require the energy of judgment, something these beings have no capability of feeling, thinking or showing. Mikail is a great friend and trusted ally. As I said before, Angels did indeed walk among us. They were the bearers of good tidings and joy.

Their teachings were not through words but through deeds. They allowed people to be people, teaching through pure love and actions, not a violent or destructive lesson, but a gentle learning.

Although they loved a great discussion and could be quite argumentative, they were on each other's side and would find themselves barracking for their opponent as well as themselves.

During the course of their stay on Earth, they became quite resilient in the ways of manipulating the Earth's energy field towards a gentler rotation. They did this through thought processes and acknowledging the overall plan of universal destiny.

Soon, the people would take notice of the Angels' antics of energy possession and began to fear them, acknowledging them as something not of themselves but rather as highly evolved beings who needed constant adoration. Before long, the Angels were being worshipped by people and to their dismay, were placed on proverbial pedestals no longer to converse with but to pray to or at. Human beings had forgotten the remembrance of the divine law, 'All is one, is One'. All teachers are learners and all learners are teachers. It is the way of life and always will be.

The Angels, acknowledging their predicament at being cast as Gods, could not continue to stay in the same vibrational structure as the humans, for once you see something separate or apart from yourself, the energy-link or connection dissipates to a lower frequency. Like dis-ease not being able to grow and evolve at a higher or lower level as itself, when human beings saw themselves as separate from the Angels (and in doing so, lowered their vibration), the two could no longer co-exist or co-evolve on the same dimension.

The Angels continued to learn, teach and grow in their own vibrational energy structure, while humans became more possessive of who the Angels were and why they were.

Some people deemed the Angels as being just for them - their own personal being to teach them enlightenment, but also to get them what they wanted through the Angels' course of miracles.

So, as the Angels maintained and evolved through their own Vibrational Molecular Structure so did humans. The only difference was that Angels continued to live as they had, with an acknowledgement of the divine source within and realization of choice and reality.

Humans, because they were looking outside themselves for the answers and forgetting their own divine intellect remembrance of who they were and why they were, began evolving and vibrating at a different molecular structure (no better or worse - just different). This then allowed the two energies (if you want to separate them), to move beyond each other, until the Angels began to be luminescent with light, then gradually became so 'light' they could no longer be viewed and/or witnessed by the human eye.

Human beings, seeing this miraculous sight, worshipped the Angels even more, allowing the mythology of greater Godlike beings who bestowed their grace and love on the world for only a short time. Again this concluded with 'we are unworthy of the full grace of God' and again 'we are alone' belief systems.

Now, the Earth's energy again is beginning to vibrate at a molecular structure coinciding with the Angelic realms. This is why there are now more sightings, more witnessed 'miracles', because I believe the human intellect is oscillating at such a rapid rate, with the realization of who we are and why we are, the

Angelic realm and Earth's energies again will 'be' as One.
I will talk more soon/tomorrow about how to witness an Angelic visit (or miracle), and how to raise your intellectual awareness to coincide with the Angelic intellect. I love you, sleep soundly. We have a lot to get through tomorrow. My love to Mum and Dad. Jason.

Jay, when did the Angels first come in contact with Earth Beings?

When the colonization of the Earth was beginning. This is what I have learnt from listening to Mikail (Archangel Michael), on our learnings and discussions together.

All planets throughout the Universe (solar system and beyond), were colonized from planets before them. In our solar system - there now being more then thirteen planets recognized - every planet itself has a divine plan. Earth rotates at its own vibrational molecular level according to its own collective consciousness and the consciousness around it.

Earth, being the 3rd planet from the Sun, has the vibrational molecular dimension of Cause and Effect.
Other planets have the molecular vibrational of positivity through acquired learning, technology through spiritual vibrational structures, technology through material vibrational structures and so on through to the 13th planet that which is oscillating to a higher (or more rapid) vibrational frequency to Earth and beyond.

Now, as I said, the planets were all colonized by other planets in our solar system.

There was a great deal of interest about Earth and her individual growth structure. Beings of another planet came forth to Earth and began utilizing Earth's productive resources of gold, copper and oil and during that project, began using their science and technology for the planets' ecosystem.

Using a highly vibrational hybrid technique, they were able to introduce a lot of their own plant life and animal life into Earth's ecosystem. In that process, they began to work on a mammal that would have intellect all its own - a part of the collective consciousness of the planet, but also apart from it.

Thus sprang the beginnings of man and woman. (I'm really glossing over this because it is not as important as the answer to your question).
T
he beings from the planet sought Spiritual Guidance from the Overseers of Pure Light and Innocence.

The Overseers were kind beings, large, tall in stature but with the energy that oscillated at a peace-filled vibration. Gentle and unobtrusive (Jay laughs "these are Mikail's words"), they've been called many names throughout history: - the "Overseers, Light-Workers, and Children of the Feather" and (more recently) Angels.

The Overseers, witnessing the hybrid of man and woman, chose to gift human beings with the energy of nonconformity, individualization, strength, honor and the GodSeed of remembrance.

So through time, the Overseers or Angels have guided our energies, explored, taught and learnt with us through quiet observation and interaction.

Mikail gives great advice on how to connect to the Angels' energy so it may resonate with yours. He says to light a candle about three hours after absorbing food. The reason for the delay after eating is that the body uses a lot of energy processing and digesting food.

When you choose your candle, any color is fine. Use your intuition. Concentrate and centre yourself in the divine knowledge of who you are and why you are. Acknowledge your divine plan with non-judgment and allow your thoughts/feelings to oscillate with the energies around you.

Slowly raise your left arm out in front of your body with your palm facing upwards and towards you (allowing yourself to acknowledge the spiritual aspect of your life).

Call forth the energy again of non-judgment and breathe in the energy of no expectations. Allow your body to relax in the energy that is being raised to a greater molecular level. Hold no thoughts in your head, only the remembrance of pure Love and Joy. Breathe in the energy of the divine plan of All is One, is One - Just breathe. The energy you are now resonating in is the energy of the Angelic realm. In darkness, the light is 'shown' (shines) stronger. It is always darkest before the dawn.

A Love Letter from a Son

Nicole, I'm so proud of you for changing the energy of your bedroom - it's a softer energy now.

Uncluttered now much to Mum's delight.

(laughs) Well she is your protector and guardian and subconsciously knows when to 'move' things to allow faster energy to move into a space where denser energy has been - now if only we can get her to believe that - truly believe that - then her healing will take place - she is resisting - as all good people do - to being selfish herself - but Mum has the very unique gift of healing others through energy - and no matter how hard she tries to squash this gift with her eating or her drinking and especially her thoughts about herself, she will never succeed in stopping that gift from happening.

Like you with your writing, it is her destiny - and what the Universe wants - the Universe gets. The only thing that is up to her is how many wonderful years of memories she will allow herself to experience, truly living and breathing her gift. It might be just a moment or a lifetime - it is entirely up to her - you and I know truly how long it will be - she just has to come to that realization herself - and want it for herself. Remember this Mum - there is no other Mother in the world that I chose to be with - I knew you would teach me about truth, integrity, compassion, security and unconditional love and you continue every moment of every day to do so - so stop being so hard on yourself - stop picking on yourself - there is no such thing as perfection - and in that imperfection you find God. You are glorious and beautiful and have such a gift of giving - so get selfish and give to yourself.

Don't you realize in healing others with vibrational healing you give to yourself? You are the channel - where else are these three dimensional beings going to get it from? And when they show up THAT'S when you truly find God - that's when you are the closest to God - you are totally connected to the Universe and all its miracles. You had cut the ties with your past yet have decided to continue the role of kicking yourself when you're down - of telling you you're not good enough - special enough - will never make anything of yourself-fuck that. Shake it off.

Create your healing room and watch people line up to enter. You love changing rooms - well do it - make 'room' for yourself now - all this energy inside you is going to build and build until you let it out - or become the good year blimp - You don't have to scream and yell to be heard - sit quietly in your room and worship yourself, to your GOD-Self, to hear yourself and watch your life become instantly happier.

You do it for Nicole but you won't do it for yourself and that's not fair to you or me. I love you so much Mum. You and Dad are always right here with me with whatever I do, whoever I help, whatever I see. After all I have Dad's strength and sense of knowing with your compassion and sense of giving. I am your Son and forever will be. (laughs) Consider this a 'son letter'.

Evolution

The human intellect is a fascinating study.

Through eons of time we have known who we were without questioning why we were. We realized or remembered, being the correct word, that we are the forbearers of our own destiny, and then something changed within us. Instead of evolving as the intellect of sophisticated spiritual beings, we (as a collective consciousness), began the evolution of sophisticated primordial material beings.

Without sensing what was happening around us, we forgot the natural and existential order of all things, all consciousness in the Universe. We began to fend for ourselves, because we began to believe that's all we were, survivors, lost and alone.
Through the survival race sprang the motto 'all for oneself'. We forgot to carry the energy of love=evolvement through with us.
We began to see power-filled people as good and righteous, and the power-full ones as dishonest and worthless.
Those of us who saw this evolvement as a chance to grow and nourish our souls with the word and light of GOD, soon became chastised and the power-filled society was repulsed by these so-called, dwellers of faith.

The dwellers of faith saw each thought, word and deed as a spiritual footstep on the path of all knowing and all accepting. Their intellect was brought forth untouched by greed of others, for they only saw each other as one of themselves.

Throughout history, the power-filled society ruled the lands and riches through either greed or corruption.

But not all were bad or wrong. Some saw this as their role as elders of the people, 'spiritual in-sighters', who had enough intellect to hear their own spiritual heartbeat throbbing inside their chest, but without the spiritual intellect or energy to look deeper within and acknowledge all are on the same path. Thus sprung hierarchy:

The overseers of society took it upon themselves to see that all that was good was treasured. Yet, they took it a little too far by hoarding the goodness and only sharing it with those who seemed worthy or those who had the nous to tell the overseers that they were worthy.
Still, the dwellers of faith remained strong... Seemingly untouched by the struggle and corruption of power, they knew (as they remembered), that all power is within and is used by the smallest molecule of sand to the largest monolith of mountains.

All is as it should be.

Moving forward:

The 1960's then sprang another source of intellect into the human existence - the struggle from power to freedom.
But this evolution left behind the hidden source of all things, the intellect of destiny and movement through balance.

So, as the world kept fighting, it also began searching for a higher evolvement in the game of life. As we came to the 1980's, the learners of the 1960's gave birth to a new collective consciousness - the consciousness of 'greed is good'(and big hair, but let's not go further into that).

It was thought that greed gets you things so much faster than Love. The consciousness sprang from itself, searching and separating until the energy became so dissipated that something had to give.
Our body's energy started breaking down. Cancer cells were dividing and accelerating their growth at a rapid pace. The world of chaotic consciousness was born.
Collective consciousness then formed the opinion that love unconditional and otherwise - was wrong. Thus sprang the AIDS virus. Love was now a disease which was spreading like wildfire. No-one was safe.

The collective consciousness had now filled a new intellect of energy of 'we're not safe', 'we need to fight to survive' and 'we really are alone'.
We have come full circle. Collective consciousness is changing. The energy is escalating to a frequency that is so rapid, so multi-faceted dimensionally, that the intellect is holding its breath, literally.
The millennium has changed us.
Collective consciousness is now moving into the **Unified Evolvement of the Collective Consciousness**. We are becoming whole.

Feeling separate was only an illusion of the intellect for the domination of power. The energy has now evolved and found its true self again.

There will never be an end of the world. There will however, be an end to this world as we now know it. The colors and energy are oscillating to such a high vibrational state that anything is possible and of course, anything is.

We no longer feel the need to hold onto the primitive consciousness of ' consciousness of ' **Survivor**'. We are now moving toward the **Unifier**'.

I see a lot of great changes happening, fascinating insights and remembrances occurring. I feel it's because human beings are taking time to stop and think about their lives, their families, themselves, who they are and where they fit into the world. Really questioning and looking **within** for the answers.
The days of asking another's advice for your life are ending. Your collective consciousness and intellect is becoming one. Opening up remembrances that have been buried deep before time.

You have the answers. The only difference between now and then is that you are all now aware that you have those answers - your own answers.

Make a conscious effort to breathe in the energized colors around you. Feel your movement of muscle, fiber and tissue and acknowledge the GOD-Seed planted so long ago in your remembrance.

It's fascinating to watch, view and take part in the ultimate consciousness of the Collective Unified Evolution of our planet.
I want to talk to you more about Passing through Time.
Firstly, there are no levels. I have not come across any energy vibration where I was not permitted or allowed to go, or bear witness to.

Secondly, there is no need to be healed or search for a light (at the end of the tunnel).

There is healing, granted. But all souls are pure, filled of light and love and the remembrance of that comes to you with your first breath of passing. It cannot do otherwise. Your mind expands and escalates at such a rapid rate that it is indeed mindblowing.

When a person has a 'near death experience', the light that people see is 100% of that experience. During a near death experience, the light that people see is actually a rapid burst of energy changing their molecular structure (mind as well as body). They themselves have called forth this light (again - choice), for a 'wake-up call', as they say. It is a common occurrence that when these people return to their physical state, they are changed dramatically in their mind, as well as belief systems and knowledge of the whole. They have a remembrance of who they are and most importantly, why they are.

These people, who have brought forward the wisdom of the energy oscillation, have not only changed their own lives, but also all those they touch and speak to, because they have lost the fear. They no longer not know. They have found their true purpose in life, which is not to teach others how to live, but of how they *were* living and *now* live. People learn by actions, not words. That's one of human emotions and intellect's biggest lessons to learn.

The people who have experienced a near death experience, accept life as it is. Not all, but most - again, choice.

They acknowledge their part in the Universal plan of remembrance and are the witness-bearers of the 'physical' re-jogging of the primordial intellect - that GOD-seed which is in-bred, in-built and never leaves us.

The ethereal plane is a dimension which oscillates one-third higher than Earth's current vibration.

Clairvoyants, mediums, visionaries and children (before the age of 7), all have the gift and intellectual insight to bear witness to this miraculous dimension - although I should correct myself....Everyone has the gift of intellectual insight to bear witness to energy dimensions. It's each person's choice to acknowledge this energy for what it is. The ethereal plane is as real as Earth, as are all other dimensions.
When you pass, you can go anywhere - absolutely anywhere you wish at just a thought/feeling's notice. There are no hierarchies in the Kingdom of Heaven. All is One, is One.

There are no lower or higher evolved spiritual beings, because we are all higher and lower, all a part of each other and besides, if you wish for higher and lower, good and evil, right and wrong, you are then acknowledging judgment at its evolving form.

There is no need for judgment. Everything is and everything is not. Remember, non-judgment is the energy of 'no expectations'. Your life is a continual surprise party! What a gift of a life that is. I love you, I am with you, and I am you - for you and I are One.

Many people will be healed with the new energy coming through with vibrational healing. Many, and soon all, hospitals will begin to see the added benefits of vibrational medicine.

Energy is science - intricate and beautiful. Energy is everything and nothing. It changes form or appearance quicker than a thought/feeling. It expands and contracts in the same instant.
Energy is its own contradiction.

Hospitals, as well as all medical facilities, will become accustomed to the healing practices of vibrational medicine. Rooms will be color-coded to the particular disease i.e. Cancer, Asthma, Leukemia, AIDS, etc, and each room will be subtle variations of the same color.

For example, if the Cancer rooms had yellow attached to the healing vibration, then there would be many delicate hues of the color yellow in these rooms.
Healers will find the intellect of remembrance and begin these healing rooms, acknowledging the vibration of a particular color and its healing properties. They will collectively remember how to raise the vibration of the room in a totally natural way, using the color for the disease.

Once people sit or lie in the room, the vibrational energy of the color will merge with their own vibrational energy and at that particular person's own pace, begin to raise the vibration of the patient to such a level where the disease cannot manifest itself in the human body at that level. It, the dis-ease, cannot continue to grow and thrive where its own energies do not match with that of the patient.

It is a well-known fact that dis-ease occurs in identical vibrational energies to itself in the patient's body. The disease ceases to exist once the body's energy levels are changed to a more frequent health-filled, energy vibration. Chemotherapy is an example of this, because it works by lowering the human body's vibration below that of the disease.

During chemotherapy, Cancer, Leukemia, AIDS, etc,. may not be detected because they exist on their own vibrational level. Once lower or higher energy levels are obtained, the dis-ease no longer exists. Chemotherapy lowers the molecular level of the human body and therefore the disease is no longer detected. The human body is now 'running' or evolving at a lower rate of vibration compared with the dis-ease. Once the patient again raises their vibrational energy level, the dis-ease reappears. If the patient still chooses to raise their vibrational molecular level to an even higher form of energy, the dis-ease is diminished because all things not evolving, (dis-eased molecular structures, blood works, white and red blood cells etc), on that particular higher level, no longer exists. Like attracts like.

The dis-eases cannot keep up with the higher frequency of the patient's molecular body vibration, so it dissipates and fails to affect the body negatively. All things in the patient's body will move/evolve with the higher vibrational molecular level.
That is the way of energy. That is its miraculous form - changing and evolving through space and time.

Self-healing of the human body, mind and soul is the most awesome discovery of eternity, towards the integration of self-acceptance, self-hope, self-faith and self-healing we'll have the majestic power of being masterful.

To master our own destinies through the awakening of selfhealing, we must come to the realization and obvious conclusion of choice.
I choose to heal.

In the self-explanation of our body, mind, soul systems we become once again aligned with the primal need for being a prosperous being which is self-sufficient.
In order to become such a being we must go towards our natural healing abilities with gentle force and care of ourselves and those around us.

The natural state of being-ness is one of exploration and explanation. To explore, question, become skeptical, and then to become one with our explanation of mindfulness, duality and realization of who we must be, in order for us to be-come.
Totaling all our previous and present experiences and lessons that we have chosen for ourselves, to come to the specific 'place' to take charge of our own health, wealth, confidence and destination of who we are individually and collectively becoming.
We will discuss each area of the mind, body, soul system, beliefs, structures and self-healing qualities, explore and ultimately explain the link between the three systems in an individual arena, and then progressively move towards the body, mind, and soul systems of the collective arena.
Once explored and explained we will then individually, as well as collectively, bring towards ourselves a more idealistic and realistic way of living, through harmonious, and vibrational techniques and mind-power affirmations for personal growth and success.

Self-Acceptance.

The right to choose is our God given right.
Choice is an intellect all its own some would say, the ultimate intellect.
Choice is destiny driven.
Every choice we make in our lives allows us the freedom and lessons we call to us to enable us to become a more successful or 'better' human being.
There are no wrong choices. Every choice we have ever made in our lives has ultimately led us to this point right now.
Every choice is a success.
Everything we have chosen to experience, to master, to fail at, to become enlightened with, was created out of a need and desire of choice.
The acceptance of Self, of who we are and why we are, is the beginning of our Journey Towards the Eternal body, mind, and soul system.
To become aware of the knowledge of our choice to come onto this Earth, as we are, physically, mentally, emotionally, we must first establish a connection with our inner world.
What makes us. What drives us. What propels us throughout our journeys.
Acknowledging the uniqueness of who we are and why we are becomes powerful in energy, because we as individuals have begun to take control.

The Inner-World.

Our body is made of energy.

Millions of electrons, and multi-functional energy plates, colliding, oscillating, disintegrating, and then reforming in an amazing kaleidoscope of vibrational and movement. The human body is movement.

When the human body is stagnating at a vibrational molecular structure, no longer oscillating around itself, but within itself, human emotions become heightened and stress is formed in and around the joints of the elbows, shoulders, hips, knees and ankles.

All these human joints are for balance and movement, their primal makings are for just that, balance and movement. So when stagnation of a life becomes a total way of life, the joints of the body begin to break down, (in a metaphysical sense).

- Thoughts cause Choice - Choice causes Movement - Movement causes Action

In changing or realigning our thought patterns, choice and movement become an instantaneous conclusion. Self-Acceptance is essential for each system of body, mind, and soul. Firstly let's look at Self-Acceptance on a body (physical) level.

We are constantly bombarded throughout our early lives, of what we should look like. Our physical appearance is always represented by either success or failure.

Constant adoration of the beauty-filled, strips the individual consciousness of the totality of balance.
Uniqueness is no longer approved, but repulsed.

We are in the age of Cloning. To become one with each other, we must first acknowledge, accept and recognize fully our own uniqueness and individualistic appearance.
No one person is more successful or less-successful to another. We all have within our body system, the balance of approval and repulsion.

It is now time to reconnect with the approval within yourself of what your physical body looks like so you can realign with the balance of the body system.

The (physical) body system will become realigned once we move toward the energy of acceptance and truth. Honest re-evaluation of yourself on a physical level allows one to become more apparent in their overall physical appearance.

To Deny Me – You Deny Yourself ♥

To Love Me – You Love Yourself ♥

To Worship Me – You Worship Yourself ♥

To Live for Me – You Live for Yourself ♥

Individual body, mind, soul systems of equality and balance. Integrating these teachings on a inward knowledge base learning will enable you, yourself to heal, to move, to choose, to live.
Firstly the individual healing of all three aspects of the body, mind, soul - physical, mental, emotions.

When first we heal individually, then and only then will we come to a better understanding of the betterment of healing collectively.

The body in three aspects of itself comes into the realization of its own full divine existence once you establish a link or connection between all and nothing.
Nothing is separate to you, as you are a part of every living thing. Your soul regeneration and activation enables you to focus on more compelling and disciplined ways of living, than you are currently living now.
For the body to reintegrate within and upon itself, first let us look at the soul level system of the body.
The most compelling attribute of the physical body is that of human emotions. Emotions (not feelings), enable us all to outwardly and inwardly express ourselves, to ourselves and to the outside world.

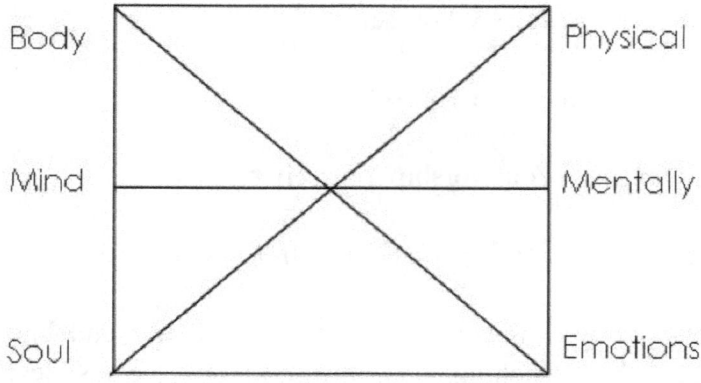

When once we begin to accept each emotion as divine and begin our discipline in acknowledging and acceptance of such emotions, we will clean and clear a lot of past issues to do with suppressed emotions. The need for suppressing any emotions comes back to a lack of self-acceptance. Unworthiness or the feeling of being wronged, or sinful comes into play. The judgment of self takes over until there is no longer self to judge. Diminished in the act of judgment and expectations, self no longer is alive or lives but merely exists. Not for itself or the love and light of its divine source, but of a confirmative nature, searching for something it never was, or never needs to be.

The respect of your self is an integral vibrational structure. In finding and reconnecting with your self-respect, you will open paths of unimaginable wonder and selfempowerment.

To reconnect with self, the respect and love of self, you must once again come into the realization of choice.

Choose to respect yourself. No longer feel the need to disgrace your own being by choosing words, feelings and actions that no longer oscillate at your own respectful vibration.

So, like disease living within its own vibration, so does honor, discipline, love and ultimately respect. Allow your image of yourself to reside in the new vibration of your being. Choose for yourself all thoughts and actions that resonate with your powerful being.

It is now time to live in your majesty. Choose respect. You will no longer draw to you vibrations that do not reside within you. Energy is energy. Like attracts like.

Respectfulness attracts respect. Acknowledging the energy of respect, truth, honor and discipline that resides with you, encourages energy to flow and attract itself in an abundant way.
If feelings of respect diminish, become aware of the knowledge that it is the energy that once surrounded you before self respect was chosen. It is a remembrance, not a choice. The energy is just vibrating at a deeper level, not less or more so, just denser. Once you become aware of these vibrational structures that are flowing around and within you, you will begin to choose, through strong thoughts, feelings and actions, the energy that allows you to fulfill your respectful choice - choice is yourself.

No longer feeling the need to disrespect yourself, you will encourage and live within that energy for eternity.
Once the choice is made, action and movement is inevitable. The only way for you to change that choice and once again exist in disrespectfulness of self, is to energize thoughts in that way.

Depending on the focus of your energy, the discipline of your actions, your choices will resonate with exactly that vibration. Like attracts like.
T
he abundance of respectful energy towards, within and around your self will become a part of your eternal makeup. For it was there in the beginning and will continuously be part of your and apart from you, but no longer separate to you.

The acknowledgment of self respect within your very being will shine forth and gravitate energy eternally as well as externally. 'Like again attracts like.'

The GOD-Seed

Jay, you speak about the GOD-Seed. What exactly is that?

It is what drives us as individuals to search for and be the best soul we can ever be. We are all part of GOD, the ultimate intellect with energy that lives within everything - every single molecule, cell and life everywhere. Nothing at all is separate from this immensely loving energy.

The GOD-Seed is such an integral part of every being. In human beings it is the energy that is located exactly on your navel, (not to be confused with your solar plexus).

It is actually embedded inside the solar plexus region. The GOD-Seed is similar to a ball of energy, always oscillating, neither right nor left, up nor down.

Once you accept who you are and begin to search for why you are, this energy then begins to activate and evolve into the time continuum symbol of eternity.

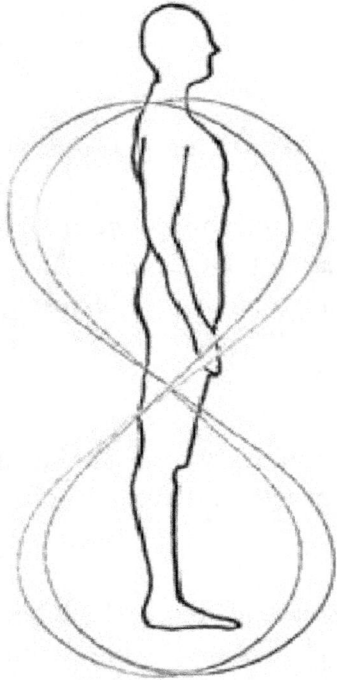

The energy evolves or moves through the root chakra, towards the back and then up to the base of the neck, down through the throat, thymus and solar plexus, then back into the root chakra in a continuing cycle.

Once the body becomes accustomed to the energy that is oscillating through, within and around it, the energy then begins to vibrate at a more rapid molecular structure. This movement initiates the start of your spiritual search (or 'quest' as we call it here where I am).

Because the body is vibrating at a more rapid, 'clearer' energy, more energy is then able to move towards, through and around it.

This in turn oscillates and generates more and more divine visions, gifts and learning. Once the being is accustomed to that energy and begins to look within more closely, the energy again surges, oscillating in rapid succession.
The GOD-Seed begins to evolve and move in greater and greater oscillations, encompassing the whole of the human body

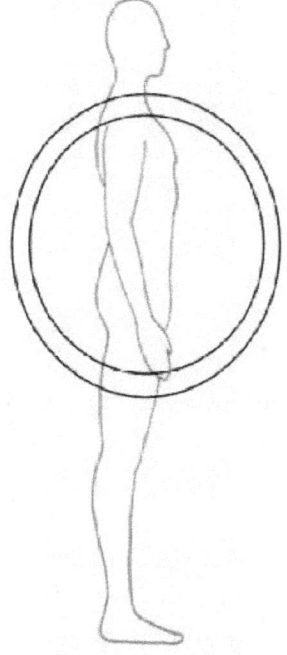

Divine search of self begins. This affects root chakra, grief point (small of back), energy of self-worth and purpose (between the shoulder blades), throat chakra, thymus, sternum and solar plexus.
Divine search begins to encompass
all life's lessons and manifestations of

thought. All of the body's central energy points oscillate at a divine vibrational molecular structure.

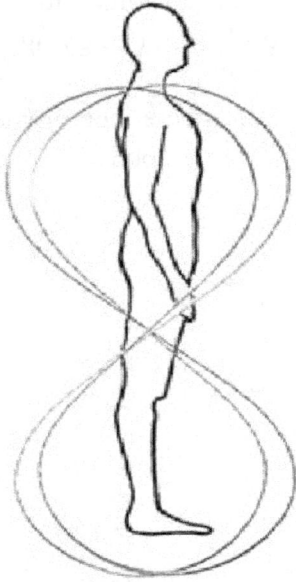

Now to begin to evolve to and move into an awareness of your GOD-Seed intellect, you need to first acknowledge the divine within your 'self'.

Practices of conscious breathing and movement enable you to recognize the body's energy and the majestic way it lives, breathes and grows. This is achieved through learning of the most integral and intricate part of energy of self.

Music plays an intricate part in reconnecting you to your GOD-Seed soul. Tribal and primitive music (e.g. African, Negro, Aboriginal, Maori), enables you to concentrate on the first stage or structure of the GOD-Seed.

The drums of the music allow you to locate the primitive energy of the GOD-Seed. Re-connection with the Earth from where you are born is the first structure of the GODSeed.

I am playing the soundtrack to the movie "Power of One". Rain has just begun to pour outside and the trees are moving with the strong wind.

Yes, connection with the Earth is important. You are born upon the Earth, but your connection with the Earth is so important.
Connection to the Earth enables the remembrance of gentle strength, letting you realize that the divine plan of ALL IS AS IT SHOULD BE (that is, in constant movement).
Through constant movement comes constant learnings and teachings. Once you re-establish your connection with the Earth, find the awe and majestic beauty that surrounds you and recognize that it also lives and breathes inside of you.

The constant drum beating and Earth chanting awakens the GOD-Seed to evolvement. Therefore, become like a child who dances in the rain. Reconnect yourself to everything, cleansing and celebrating, moving and oscillating with the energy around you. Allow the energy to move through and around your body, recognizing and being in awe of the majestic energy of freedom which fills your very being.

Once through discipline and practice you have begun to establish the re-connection of remembrance within yourself, you will then evolve (and move) into a newer, cleaner energy.

During the practice of conscious breathing and movement (achieved through Tai Chi, Chi Gung and other similar arts), you will feel a shift begin. Old thoughts and feelings will resurface which have lain dormant in your solar plexus.

The energy you are now working with (and not against, as you may have been), searches for energy vibrations like itself. As this energy revitalizes the root chakra and the grief point, you will find 'movement' occurring in various issues in your life. This could be to do with sexual issues and memories moving through to grief issues, the energy begins to oscillate through the small of your back, resurfacing remembrance that you are indeed not alone and letting go of old ideas of who you are and what the world is.

The energy then evolves to the area between your shoulder blades. Feelings and thoughts of your self-worth and purpose in your own life and others will surface. Allow all feelings to come. Remember no feelings are good or bad - only feelings.
Once the energy is cleaner and clearer, the GOD-Seed then moves through to the base of your neck. Feelings and thoughts about your connection with yourself and family comes into progress of a spiritual nature. An acknowledgment of the learning and teachings of all paths, with no-judgment and no-expectations, begins to move through your entire soul.

As the energy once again becomes cleaner and clearer, it then evolves to the throat area. Feelings of stifled conformity surface and the energy begins to vibrate at a different molecular structure.

Your voice may become softer, yet stronger due to the energy. Allowing yourself to speak about your experiences, feelings, movements, and thoughts will then enable a 'cleaner' energy to resonate within yourself.

Energy then moves to the sternum at the front of your body. Feelings of guilt re-surface as well as selfconsciousness and stress. Allow these feelings and thoughts, which are congested in this area, to re-surface. This will bring on the energy of release and uninhibited awe.

The energy then moves through to the solar plexus.

Feelings and thoughts about lost opportunities and misjudged experiences surface. Allowing the energy of these issues to re-surface enables you to clear and become confident again of your body's natural ability to sense or predict experiences that will ensure growth of your individual intellect.

As the GOD-Seed evolves through the body, allow all feelings and thoughts to come to the surface. This will ensure that you are resonating with the energy of the GOD-Seed.

The GOD-Seed, if you have a need to visualize, is seen as a golden orb, brilliant in light and oscillating at an infinite vibrational structure - It never diminishes. One area of the body is not brighter than the other. The color does not change - for it is all colors and none.

However, if you do visualize a color, take notice of the color and feel how the color resonates with you.

Remember - darker colors are not negative, nor are bright, positive. All is One, is One.

Now once the GOD-Seed has oscillated through these particular energy structures within the body and the energy has become cleaner and clearer, the energy then begins its rapid formation of growth.

The GOD-Seed begins to expand, allowing new experiences to become drawn to this particular energy field. In this expansion comes great movement and within this movement, comes greater awareness of the body's Soul purpose or desire of intellect -

First stage of GOD-Seed oscillation Structure.

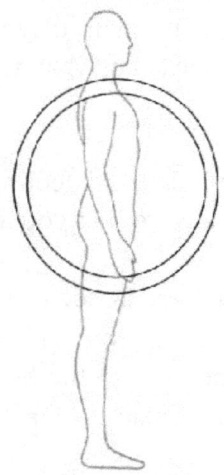

Second stage of GOD-Seed oscillation structure.

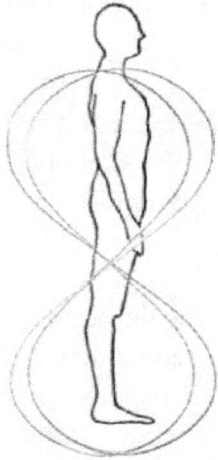

The second stage of the GOD-Seed oscillation structure moves, (or moves into), the energy points of the body's vibrational structure.

Still evolving through the sacral, lower back, shoulder blades, throat, sternum and solar plexus areas, the GODSeed stretches or evolves into a larger area, always obtaining new energy and experiences.

These new areas include the thighs, knees, ankles and feet of the human body.

Notice that these physical structures are what allows you to move forward, backward and sideways. They are also your body's way of showing you the primal need of balance within and around your life.

Once the GOD-Seed becomes one again with its natural self, (the GOD-Seed placement centre in the solar plexus region), the energy (intellect), then evolves through the thigh area of the body.

Feelings of strength and individualization will come to the surface. A large portion of self-worth issues are held in your knee and ankle area.

Your thighs represent the feelings of self-empowerment and self-control. Overall balance is maintained by the GODSeed evolving through, within and around your thigh area. The overall balance pertains to your life and how you judge it.

You may feel cramps in your thighs and your sciatic nerve (an unconscious control point of movement), will become activated and, in most cases, agitated. Allow the feelings of free movement to sweep through your thighs as you gather strength through knowledge and self-worth.

Now, the GOD-Seed evolves through, within and around the knee area. Feelings of restricted direction (in emotions and the living of our lives), are stored. The feelings of 'not aspiring to the best of your ability' bring through the energy of conformity, stagnation and procrastination.

Allow all feelings, memories and emotions to come to the surface. Remember no feelings are good or bad - just feelings.
The GOD-Seed then evolves through, within and around the shins and ankles. Again we store emotional issues of conforming to others' opinions of our life in this area.

Your ankles hold this key of flexibility and learning through directional balance and movement. Allow the pure energy of self-expression through 'taking charge' of responsibility of your life's direction.

Next, the GOD-Seed moves to your feet. Here it circles and embraces itself through the knowledge of self-power and realistic memories and dreams of your own life. Your feet are your grounding energy. They are what connects you to the realization of who you are and what you are becoming. The feet store memories of intellect bias, through conformity and lack of good judgment. The energy of having lived your life as you see fit.

When the GOD-Seed evolves/moves through the feet, it reawakens the primal need for connection and stability in your life. Once feelings of such emotions have been cleaned and cleared, the GOD-Seed moves through, within and around the back of the leg, encompassing the calf muscles, the back of the knee joint and the hamstrings. All of these energy structures in the body are interconnected with issues or feelings of gentle movement. Stiffness is the result of over-compensation and the need to conform to other people's opinions about your life. By clearing these emotional blockages, you will find a resurgence of gratitude for other people's actions and will re-establish empowerment of movement in your own life and lifestyle.

The GOD-Seed then evolves through, within and around the buttocks. Here, stifled emotions are stored in relation to severe loss of self-worth. This area also registers issues which relate to holding onto instead of moving through, with the creativity and the character of the embodied soul (your personality). The buttocks are close to the grief spot and enable you, through creative practices, to move into the feelings, thoughts and emotions of strength, balance and self-acknowledgement.

Once the GOD-Seed intellect has become one with its natural self, the GOD-Seed begins to oscillate at a more rapid vibrational structure. Similar to the first and second stage of remembering and clearing the emotions, thoughts and feelings of self-esteem, balance and movement (directional and emotional) will re-surface.

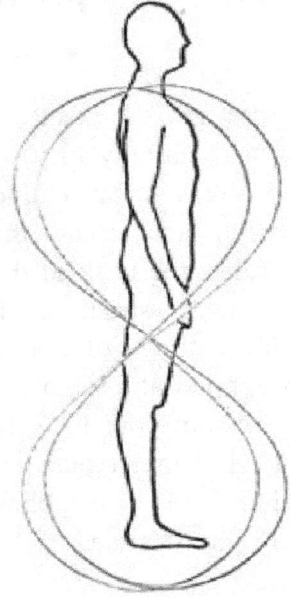

The third stage begins to envelop the intellectual molecular structure of the soulbody. This stage envelops or evolves to and into, the molecular structure of the breath channel (the third eye, crown and over-soul portion of the human body).

With the GOD-Seed expanding its energy (intellect) through the body's central nervous system and the energy centers within and around the body, the THIRD stage (or structure) evolves, through, in and around the breath channel.

This breath channel is located above the throat energy centre (or chakra as it is widely known), encompassing the jawbone, mouth, nose and sinus area of the body.

Feelings of restricted emotions or self-confronting emotions are primarily held in these energy centers of the human body. The sinus area is a centre which enables the freeflowing of emotions, allowing the body to eliminate mucous (or congested emotions). Blocked sinuses symbolize unshed tears.

The GOD-Seed evolves through all the energy centers of the breath channel simultaneously. When the energy of the breath channel is cleared and cleaned, the GOD-Seed then evolves through, into and around the third eye centre. This centre establishes the soul's desire for inward expression of the outward life being lived, i.e., visions of a celestial and/or intellectual structure occur.

The third eye is the remembrance energy structure of the human body. The link between the GOD-Seed primal centre and the third eye structure of the human body, when established, is an integral symbol of the human connection to the GOD-Within and the GOD-Without (the GOD outside of self).

Feelings of nausea and tension headaches or migraines are an established physical link with the GOD-Seed reconnection with the third-eye. Feelings of how 'small' you are, compared to the outside world, will resurface.

The divine plan of reconnection with all things great and small has an important remembrance with the human body's ability to comprehend the intellect in its entirety.

Reconnecting with the feelings and thoughts that 'nothing is impossible' and 'there is more to living than the life I have previously been living', allows the GOD-Seed energy to oscillate at a rapid vibrational molecular structure. Images of light flashes and colours will become visible around material and physical structures. Once focused upon and learnt, these insights will help with the body's own healing.

Next, the GOD-Seed proceeds to the crown energy structure of the human body. Located in the middle of the skull, this energy's primal structure is for the releasing or elimination of unused energy that the body, soul and GODSeed generate.

Cleaning and clearing this energy structure enables the insight of abundant health throughout the body. Feelings and thoughts related to constriction (and the restricted use of the body's energies), will resurface.

Through re-balancing and remembrance of the GOD-Seed and the primordial flow of that energy, these restrictions may be cleaned and cleared. As a result, the life of the individual will be able to vibrate or gravitate to a less dense energy and health will improve (through intellect and remembrance). A pure sense of self and divinity will emerge. Therefore, you can see, that this is the flow or evolution of the GOD-Seed soul. By remembering always that the soul encompasses the body (the body does not encompass the soul), you will be led to a more direct sense of health, well-being and self-control in your life and your destiny.

Remember also that the GOD-Seed's evolution is ever growing and ever-lasting.

No soul is without a GOD-Seed, and no soul is purer or cleaner than another. The particular evolvement of your GOD-Seed is as individual as your breath.

Through all of eternity the GOD-Seed is evolving and moving into less and less dense energy, always finding and remembering the divine plan and that of the individual's divine plan.

Remember also, that the GOD-Seed's primordial color is that of none and all. This is not to be confused with the colors (and vibrational molecular structure) of the energy centers through, within and around the body (the chakras).

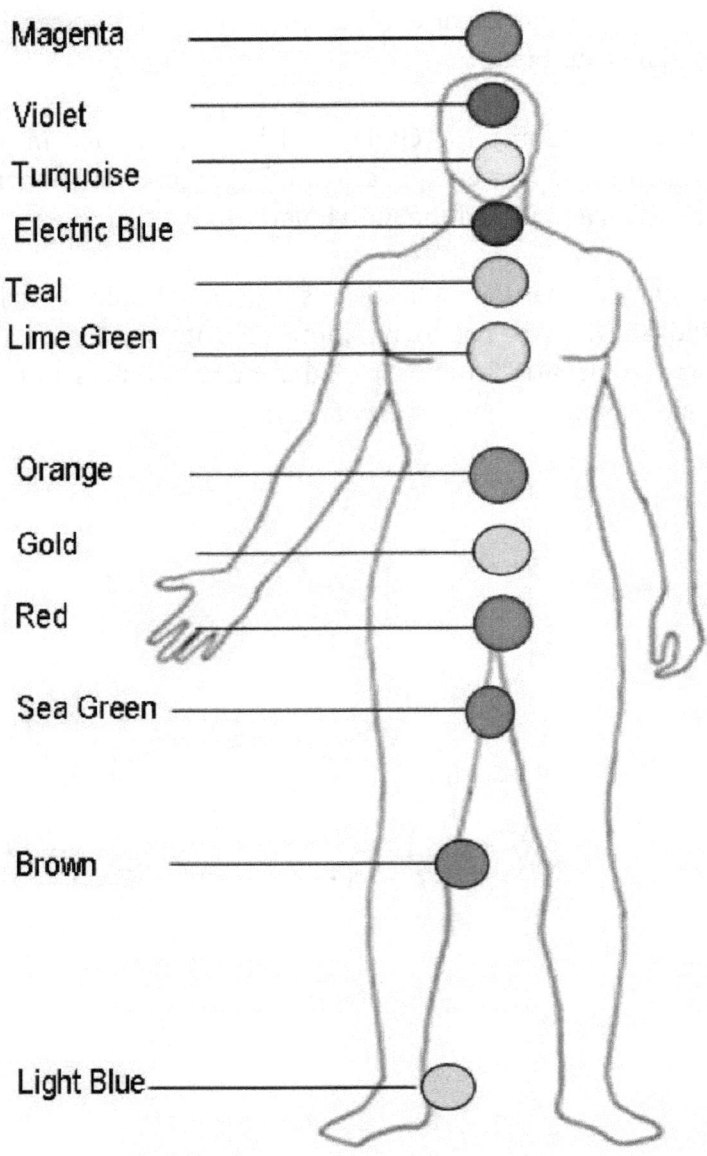

These colors or chakras are ever changing and ever oscillating in vibration color wheels. Once you breathe in, the colors become more dense and brighter. Once your breath is released, the colors become less dense and pastel in hue (color).

The wheels (energy centers), oscillate in every direction depending upon the individual and what needs to be learnt in the physical. The wheel may feel or be visualized going clockwise or anti-clockwise. Neither is right or wrong, but indeed perfect for that individual.

Grief Spot situated at small of Back

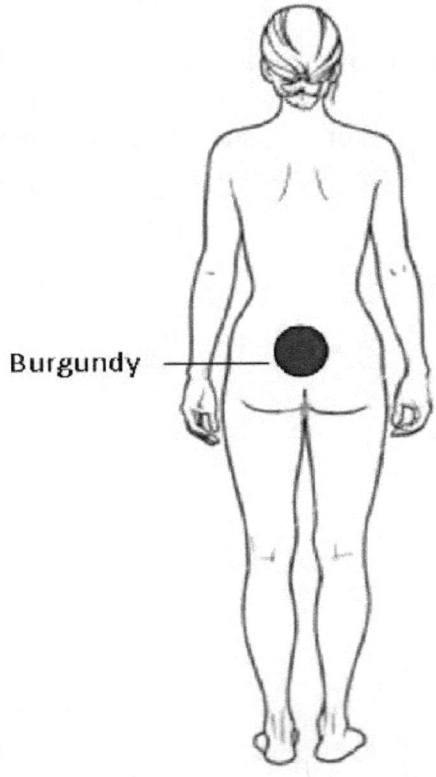

Burgundy

Once the realization of the GOD-Seed is established or remembered, the energy wheel begins to oscillate (move into), the vibration of the GOD-Seed. Again, the direction of movement is not to be judged. Neither left, right, up or down is considered more or less evolving than the other.

Once the GOD-Seed is embedded into the individual growth patterns and the individual Vibrational Molecular Structure is established and oscillating at a rapid vibration, the energy structures (chakras) begin to evolve into the colors of all. All colors oscillate at every energy structure, enabling the energy of intricate colors to weave into the movement of the GOD-Seed.

Again, once this structure of remembrance and reconnection is established, the breath of the body oscillates the colors of energy. Breathing in, the colors become more dense/brighter and by releasing the breath, the colors become less dense/pastel in hue.
We are all immortal. Every living organism on this Earth, indeed included in this Universe, has survived and reached immortality.

Our memory-based intellect has evolved to such an awesome power that lives, locations, rituals, experiences; memories are recorded in everyone's blueprint. If you are affected by anything, you have reached immortality. You are evolved into it. There has never been a search for immortality, for immortality has never been lost, nor has it ever been something to look up at, but merely was evolved at in a particular time and space.

Everything that is born of energy - whether that is dense, fragmented or pure energy, has evolved into its own immortality. Energy has trace patterns that vibrate at a particular rate, differing from all others. Like human DNA, this energy is unseen by the eye, cannot be touched (therefore cannot be taken), but can be tapped into.

Once focused upon, the energy of anything can be brought forward to a particular time and space, tapped into and harnessed so information and technology will never be lost but grow, as it is continuing to do at such a rapid state in the early 21st Century. Why? Because humans' DNA is changing to a more constant emotional, unified consciousness.

Like atoms in a cell separate, they energize themselves, their surroundings, harness together, vibrating at the same speed, same rate, they now effect and affect everything. Once only using one third of its own true power, now generating power at a phenomenal rate, affecting itself, stimulating power, growing, vibrating as 'free energy'.

If you are remembered you are Immortal.
Photographs, recorded messages, video, and memories, link immortality to a particular place, to a particular person. On a more metaphysical level looking beyond material, physical anomalies, fingerprint, aromas, smells, DNA, energy transference patterns, all can be traced, all can be tapped into, to learn from, teach from, a sound base of facts of memories, now your own, stimulating intellect, causing experiences, memories.
Remembered learning's create Immortality.

Ok. Can you now explain to me about there being 'no time'. How does that happen? How do you explain history if there is no time?

Oh, (feel that Jay is rubbing his hands together). This is such a confused subject with one of the easiest explanations that I have come across.
Ok. Humans' think of time as linear - like getting from A to B. Realization then forms that there is a distance from A to B and they naturally call that 'time'.
Now without the realization of time, how do you live your life?

Try it - I urge you to try it for a day. No watches, no clocks, no television, no radio, no music (your mind subconsciously counts the beats of music, enabling you to reconstruct a time formation). See how long your day feels. With the exception of no music, this is how we should all be living.

The saying that 'there is no time', has been taken literally for a long time (pardon the pun). Time is not literal. Time is irrelevant. Choice and learning is relevant, whereas the timing of such choices, learning and growth is not.

So, with the voice of many saying 'there is no time', try not to take it literally. Many people who have channeled this information have yet to receive the final part of the statement. There is no time - like the present.

Meaning 'live in the now'. Do not fear choices or change - they enable movement and growth. They are exciting, wonderful structures of life.

Too much damage is being done to the subconscious by transmitting the news bulletins. There is no need for people to know about what is taking place on the other side of the world, or to feel guilt, anger or hatred for these events. Once you no longer feel 'tied' to the television or radio news bulletins, I assure you that your life will be 'on an even keel'.

Live your life through your own CHOICES. This is so important. Do not pay attention to the linear clock. Live by your own metabolic clock. You know your life's choices and the lessons to be learnt from such choices. Do not hold onto the 'timing' of such choices.

Remember, you can never be too late and you can never be too early.
You are always - always, Right on Time.

Abundance

Why is it that our dreams never seem to come into our reality quick enough? And when they do, it seems too late so we are blasé about them?

Dreams are thought processes of energy that accumulate and grow to such a sizeable amount that they become dense and molded together until they form a tangible idea. The idea then changes in energy frequency depending on the needs and desires of those that are processing the energy (i.e. the dreamer or the wishmaker)... Once the idea becomes so filled with energy, including hopes, fears and realizations, it then seems to be a touch-based realism. You can almost touch and taste it it is that close.

Now the human emotion of wanting so badly for that idea, dream or wish to come true, actually repels it to a safe distance. SO close to visualize, but too far away to actually grab hold of.
We feel safer when it's there. We can then be accustomed to the energy of wanting but not receiving, which gels with one of the most primordial instincts known to man - the feeling of unworthiness or not being worthy. Notice the people around you who seem to 'have it all'.

They 'have it all' because they have broken through the barrier, stepped through the gate and grabbed their dreams by the throat and haven't let go (a harsh visualization I know, but also true).
The most simple advertising slogan known to man, which will rarely be beaten is "Just do it".

Just do your dream, wish or desire. Nothing is holding you back. No-one is holding the dream, wish or desire away from you but yourself. Humans have the rare intellect of visualizing strongly their dreams, wishes, etc,. but when it comes to the crunch they back away. waiting for someone to take it from them or saying, "No...you can't have it because you don't deserve it".

Try this.
Write every dream, wish, and desire on a piece of paper. Fill a whole journal if you like. Leave a column on the left side of the page, (left being spiritual side). In the column, write down the reasons why the dream or wish or desire is obtainable. On the right hand side (right being your physical), write down exactly why you can't have it. You'll be amazed at how quickly that right side column will fill with excuses for you not to have what you wish for.

In this exercise you will begin to take charge of your own life, realizing no-one is stopping you from doing anything you want or need to do for yourself, but yourself.

Jay, why do some people have a lot of riches and others like myself struggle almost daily?

Because it's where your perspectives lie Nicole. People who have riches and wealth do so for themselves. We are all born the same. We come into this world with nothing materialistic at all.
Now it's true that some are 'born into' money, but please don't think that they have it made. Most of the time those people struggle all their lives to establish their own identity, their own individualism. It can be the most imprisoned life a person could ever live - if they allow it.

But let's talk about you as an example.
You have been affirming for years that you will have 'more money then you will ever need'.

yes

...but don't you find you always have? When bills have come in haven't you always been able to draw money to you with a little left over?

but that's not what I meant when affirming.

But that's exactly what your actions have stated. You affirm to yourself that statement yet you don't visualize what you are affirming and your actions don't back their plan up either.
Ok. Let's put it in simpler terms. What are you going to do with your riches?

Give some to Mum and Dad, pay off debt, go on holidays, buy fancy car, give to charity, buy a house where family and friends can live, buy friends' houses, set some up in their own business.

So why wouldn't the Universe just cut out the middle man and give it straight to them?

huh?

You state you're going to give to charity, give to family, give to friends - but what are you giving to yourself Nicole?

house, holiday, car, pay off debts.

Well that can all be done with four hundred thousand dollars. So with your affirmation of 'more money than I will ever need' that is exactly what you are getting. If you got a windfall of money - in your current mindset you will be the poorest rich girl in 6 months. The Universe is just cutting out the middle man - you - and giving it directly to those you are affirming about because they have something that you currently don't.

what?

The Belief that they Deserve It.

Remember. The Universe helps those that help themselves. This is not a cruel law. It is a Universal Law. Simpler terms. In nature if you were a lion you would starve to death within days because you would continue to 'feed' the family and friends first and just be grateful for any scraps.
Get selfish Nicole. Affirm that you are getting the money because you are worth it, you deserve it, and it's in your Universal plan to receive it. Once you have the money, then give it to yourself. Do what makes you happy first.

what if giving it to family and friends makes me happy?

Well if that was the case Nicole, you would be ecstatically happy right now instead of stressing about how to pay your bills.
You're still in the mindset that if you give to others you will be liked and loved and looked after, thought of as a nice person etc. But money has absolutely nothing to do with what people think of you. DO you hang out with your friends because of their bank balance?

I have no idea what they have in the bank.

Exactly! You hang out with them because when you're with them you feel good about yourself - you literally at times feel 'like a million dollars' don't you? Is it because of what they have spent on you? No. It's because the greatest most precious gift you could give someone is the energy to allow them to be themselves without judgment or ridicule. Knowledge and love. The greats Universal gifts of all. And when you give to someone those gifts, it is priceless.

So start affirming to the Universe that you are getting this money for yourself because you deserve it. You're worth it. And spoil yourself when you get it. Don't ever think people will be jealous or try to rip you off (because of course, affirm that enough times and it will happen).

Affirm to the Universe that your friends and family will be happy for you. That they will then see and say 'if she can do it I can too'.

When you're affirming this with every breath, when your actions are living this, when your mindset is unwavering, then and only then will you receive the windfall you are thinking of.

Weight Loss

Jay, why is it so hard for so many people to lose weight? Some struggle with their weight loss journey for years. How do some people stay fit and healthy and others become rapidly obese?

I'm going to have to answer that question in several parts. Firstly let's start being in the mindset that everything is energy. Breathe that in. Vibrate in that. How do you feel? (Lighter, clear in thought, peaceful yet energized).
Now in that energy visualize yourself being the healthiest, happiest and fittest person you know you can be.
Because that's one of the main traps for people who have issues with their weight. I call them 'issues' Nicole not 'weight journeys' for a reason.

An issue implies that there is a total mental block on a situation you are currently dealing with. A 'journey' is an adventure that some people have their whole lives. Similar to a roller coaster ride their journey takes them through highs (reaching goals), lows (putting the weight back on), twists and turns (physical ailments to slow weight loss down such as a 'twisted ankle' or 'turned kneecap', 'twisted vertebrae' etc), exhilaration (the initial visualization of finishing at goal weight) and fear (lack of belief that they can ever reach their goals).

And like any roller coaster it starts off really slow until you hit the highest point, then it's all downhill from there until you come to a sudden stop (putting the brakes on everything and giving up completely).

Therefore if you're serious about 'dropping the weight' stop calling it a 'journey'. Energy is energy and you draw to you situations, people, places, things with your thoughts, be they conscious or subconscious.
Now people with a weight problem, be it over-weight or underweight, must begin to deal with their issue subconsciously. Listen to what you're saying to yourself or about yourself in your mind.

Becoming aware of your thoughts as they happen has such a rapid vibration attached to it that it only sets you up in life to great things. Therefore listen to your thoughts and begin to 'see' what you're telling yourself (self loathing, not good enough, stupid, worthless etc,).

Now remembering that words have vibrations and remember how we spoke about words with a denser vibration and how you felt. Let's go in that mindset briefly.
Now think about food. What's the first thing you thought about when you said the above dense energy words?

Potato chips and chocolate

Ok good. Now tell yourself great words, words that are filled with rapid vibration, words such as *Phenomenal, Passion, Love, Excitement, Exuberant, Adventure, Greatness and Destiny!* Now, think about food. What was your instant thought?

a juicy green apple ... laughs

Exactly Nicole!

When you tell yourself high rapid vibrational thoughts there is no way that your body would want to be fuelled by a denser energy source such as processed foods. It will naturally gravitate; move you towards only those foods that will continue that high rapid vibration within it. And why? Because it feels great. It feels amazing.

When you feel energized you feel like you could conquer the world, do a triathlon, run a marathon etc,.

When your thoughts are vibrating at a rapid rate with words of such positive force, it is like you have become a magnet for great things. The sun seems to shine brighter, colors appear luminescent, you see amazing brand new sports cars on the road, people everywhere are smiling, and you walk past a group of young people laughing and enjoying life. Your life becomes a Disney animated movie. Your life becomes EXACTLY what it was meant to be.

Therefore, change your thoughts by changing your dialogue. Grab a piece of paper and write down every word you can think of that is a 'high rapid vibrational' word. Get a thesaurus if you need to. Write down a hundred words.

Make three copies. Now put one page on your fridge door, one in your cupboard and one on your bathroom mirror.

Now every time you see the list you say five (5) words out loud. Sing them. Shout them. Have passion in your voice when you say them.
Fill the room up with excitable energy.

Then see what foods you reach for, see what words and thoughts you say to yourself when looking in that bathroom mirror after saying those high rapid vibrational words.

Become the change you want to see on the outside by exciting the inside (soul, spirit) enough to change its vibrational energy to belief, faith, laughter, happiness, joy and love and not self-loathing, hatred, fear.

Banish those words from your outside dialogue and soon your inner dialogue won't go towards them, instead automatically gravitating towards only high rapid vibrations.

Now when truly in that vibration, with those words swarming around in your head, think 'how do I feel and what do I want to do'?

I feel great, actually feel thin and want to take puppy for a walk then ride my bike; which is weird because its 11:30pm ... laughs

(laughs) Exactly! So now can you see that there is no need for diets, supplements, pills, potions etc?
All you need to do to lose weight is change your inner dialogue.

Your energy will shift, gravitating you towards livelier more energizing, nutritious foods as well as making you physically want to move.

5 words each time you see that list. It will soon become an automatic response whenever you enter those rooms. Then get crazy, go wild. Say 5 high rapid vibrational words whenever you enter ANY room.

Imagine the possibilities that will automatically attract? Imagine going to work, and as soon as you enter, say those 5 words. Even if it is in the course of conversation.

How are you? *I'm Phenomenal, Awesome, I'm full of Joy* (hell, if the Marines can say it why can't you?) *I'm Excellent, I'm Loving today.*

That's 5. How many times do you get asked a day how you are? Think about the words that you're not only telling yourself, but others and more importantly the Universe. Think about when you get home from work, what is the first thing you reach for the most?

cigarettes, packet of chips and coffee

Dense foods are linked with dense energy. Remember - Like Attracts Like. Change your inner vocabulary to powerful words, and watch yourself reach for those high fuelled rapid vibration foods ... And just try and stop yourself wanting to move - I bet you can't. I love you. Jay.

Just finished watching the finale of 'The Biggest Loser', What an inspiration people are!

And that just goes to show what happens when you focus all your energy on a goal and you keep that momentum (energy) going in everything you do. But most importantly, everything you think. Your thoughts ARE actions. What you think manifests in your life.

Your thoughts ARE actions - thoughts are energy at one of its purest forms. So what have you been thinking about that has manifested Nicole?

I'm ugly, fat and alone.

And what has happened lately Nicole?

I've put on weight, my skin has broken out and my romantic relationships are non-existent.

There you go. Your thoughts are what attract you to circumstances (situations) in your life - if you focused on positive more empowering thoughts what has happened?

I've stood up for myself and felt completely secure in who I am. I have realized I have to do it for myself and not others. I didn't 'settle' for crap or I'll talk about myself. I have found unlimiting amount of belief in myself. I've worked out my finances and paid all my debts out and feel great. I have started our new book with you and realized it's only days 'till my life changes dramatically, magically.

Now isn't that much better to focus on, to think about?

Definitely!

How do you feel when you think about the words ugly, fat, alone, worthless?

Exactly that...I feel exactly those things.
And how do you feel when you think about the words unlimited belief, greatness, and magic, secure, powerful?

Again exactly those words.

Ok, then so maybe, just maybe, do you think that words have energy no matter what context they are used in? Think about it. Powerful. Unlimited Belief. Magic. Secure. Selfish - selfish is not a negative word. Selfish is one of the most mis-used words in the English language. To be selfish is to be seen to be greedy, uncaring, unloving, manipulative even hateful. Yet being selfish, truly being selfish is just putting yourself first. You were so right the other day when you said 'The Universe looks after those that look after themselves first".

Why do you think that statement is so powerful? Because YOU are the Universe. YOU are not separate from, but a part of it. So in putting yourself first you are firmly stating to the Universe (yourself/energy) that you finally get it, you finally have worked out 'the secret'.

That's the one thing that movie didn't state too clearly. Remember Sai Baba used to say 'come to me as a child?' Children know no other way than to be selfish. If they are hungry, they ask for food, thirsty -drink, cold - warmth. Therefore be childlike and just know like a child that you will get what you know you deserve.

But what if I feel I deserve unworthiness, loneliness and bankruptcy?

Then you're up shit creek aren't you?

Ummm thanks ...

Remember we spoke about energy and how it moves throughout the body like a figure 8?

Yes.

Well when you use limiting words such as the ones you used that energy becomes stuck in a 'one track' system. In other words, instead of the energy moving through you in a multi dimensional state it begins to slow and become dense, almost sluggish, beginning to move only in a fourth and third dimensional state (fourth dimension being one of complete feeling, third dimension being one of physical denseness).

That's why you feel it in your physical being more predominately than any other state of being. This also makes use of the saying 'one track mind'.

Your thoughts begin to move you towards situations, people and experiences that match that 'one track mind' kind of thinking. The simplest way to change that is to quite literally change your 'mind'.

Move yourself towards a more lucrative state of being by choosing to think words that have a faster (not better or higher) but faster vibrational energy. And in an instant, faster vibrational energy will gravitate towards you and it to them. We are all energy. Pure and Simple.

Relationships

Jay, why is it so hard to find a partner? Is there such a thing as a soul mate?

You are so strong in your belief system Nicole your morals and integrity are high, but so are your expectations of others. You are so strong and independent that you find it hard when others need to lean on someone, need to find companionship in people that you know aren't 'good' for them. And you become too quick to dismiss anybody that suddenly shows human attributes such as fear, apprehension, obsession or jealousy.

Once you understand that you aren't perfect as you perceive yourself to be you will begin to let these 'mere mortals' into your energy and might even have the best adventures of your life.

So you're saying it's my fault then?

Yes and no. You meet these people and initially find them attractive, funny etc,. but once you become friends with them and they show you they are as insecure (as you think you aren't), you lose all attraction for them. Everybody has faults Nicole; nobody is perfect, so nobody is the 'perfect' one for you. Ask any couple that have been together longer than 10 years. Even ask Mum and Dad and they will tell you that they never thought they would end up with someone like each other but thank God they did.

Give these people a chance Nicole. Allow them their mistakes and their imperfections and just have fun with them.

So ... where was the 'and no' part of that scenario?

It's all as it should be. Your choices are neither, good nor bad, right nor wrong.

... yeah.! Way to make me feel better...

Your partner is just around the corner now because in me telling you all this today your energy has shifted slightly into a more loving, more non-judgmental energy that will allow your lovers to be drawn to you.
Funny thing is you're non-judgmental when it suits you. It's not a game show Nicole. Life is an adventure. I think you lost sight of that somewhere.

Your death and my failed relationships maybe??

Well my passing was destined. None of us could have stopped that and your relationships were doomed from the beginning.

Bloody hell Jay ... (laughs) ... thanks

You know this Nicole. It's not exactly a surprise to you or the Universe. You ignored the 'warning bells', signs and more importantly your intuition *every single step of the way.*

You were so much stronger than them in every aspect, including what it means to be truthful, and true to yourself. But stop thinking that every person you come into contact with from now on is going to be that person again. You label them as such before they get the chance to prove otherwise.

Why did I have the relationship with them if it was destined to be doomed from the beginning?

Because at the time it was fun? You're losing sight of it Nicole. You can make mistakes. And sometimes those mistakes are the best times of your life.

Don't look at relationships ending as failed - look at them as one amazing adventure that moves you into another. Chill out and stop being so serious. Since when did you give a shit about what anyone thought anyhow?

Plus...stop putting other's feelings ahead of your own. You do it so much in your life, with affirming of money, to your career, to your friendships and relationships. And when all is said and done you're not doing anything. Just have fun, Nicole.
Let your hair down (laughs) and live every moment like it was meant to be. Every moment is destined.

Even the boring ones?

But they don't have to be boring; you can find fun and adventure in every moment. Stop worrying about your friends' feelings so much - because when it comes down to it, they sure as shit aren't going to worry about yours if a partner comes along, so grab each adventure with both hands and see where they take you. Stop worrying so much.

I didn't think I was.

Well your energy is that of apprehension, but you see it as something to brace yourself against instead of just embracing it. Go for it Nicole. Go for all of it. Don't let anything bring you down. Don't let anyone force your hand. And just enjoy every part of the process... even the perceived yucky bits.

Meditation and Visualizations

The following article was an essay I had written for Quantum Knowledge Magazine exactly 2 weeks before the sudden passing of Jason.

'Living through Grief'.

Many of us in one part of our lives or another, have been through some form of grieving. It may be a loved one who has passed suddenly, or the suffering of a close friend. Yet there are other more subtle forms of grief that you may be going through without being aware that you are in the grieving stage in your life. This may be experienced as loss of friendship, loss of job, loss of loyalty or loss of control.

Loss of Friendship
Personally, this is one of the hardest to move through. Other than the death of a loved one, loss of friendship remains raw for a very long time due to the person or persons who remain still in your life in some from.

The symptoms you may suffer are similar to that of the death of a loved one; sleeplessness, lack of appetite, anger, confusion, but also disillusionment, feelings of betrayal and slight paranoia.
You may go through serious bouts of depression and anger and believe it or not, these are all good emotions. You must allow yourself to feel them fully and then 'let them go'.

Grieving allows the body to move through the anger and pain at a healthy emotional level. Firstly, it allows you to rediscover that you are a deeply sensitive human 'being'. Secondly, it allows the body to flow through its natural stream of emotions and thirdly, it allows you to break down the boundaries and re-adjust your life or lifestyle.

Like that of a steady summer rainstorm, allow the feelings of grief to flow and sweep through you. Try not to build boundaries and walls around the emotions like a huge black umbrella, but allow the waves of emotion to be and flow through their natural cycle.

Remaining strong and in control is an illusion, for being strong is recognizing the body's resourcefulness of adaptability and power. You will find that once you flow through the emotions, the feeling of being in control changes its meaning to a letting go of anger and resentment and coming around full circle to the energy of unconditional love of oneself.

We are emotional beings. Every moment of our lives, we are re-evaluating our emotions and feelings in one form or another. Allowing ourselves to move deep inside of our emotions, to feel...then to let go, is the strongest and healthiest way to cope with the grieving process. The energy of letting go is one of true Discipline and Mastership. In the act of letting go, you must allow yourself to feel every emotion as it occurs, otherwise blockages or boundaries, emotional as well as mental, occur.

Once you have moved through the emotions of anger, self-pity etc,. you no longer need to feel or put yourself through the self-doubting psychoanalysis. You have moved on and out of that energy and you no longer need to draw to yourself similar lessons.

It also enables you to remember circumstances and memories of what the body felt like when you were going through the experience as you have already lived it fully.

Visualization helps greatly in the grieving and letting go process. Like the afore-mentioned scene of the summer storm and the umbrella, visualize yourself sitting in the middle of a perfect field. Your perfect field.

You notice clouds; let them come. Do not fear them for they are your cleansing and re-birthing...our remembrance. Notice the sky. What colors are shown? Are there others around you or are you alone?

Notice the clouds now becoming thick and heavyset across the sky. Again, notice their colors. Is there lightning or thunder? See then the droplets of rain. Where first do they land? Are they hard and fast or like soft dew falling? Also notice the angle of the rain. Is it coming from the left, right or straight from above?
Now allow yourself to feel. Gently refrain from putting any boundaries or walls around you or above you, you are safe. Nothing can harm you. You are cleansing, freeing yourself of all anger and self-judgment, of all disappointment.
Now allow yourself to shed your own tears. Do they fall like the rain or differently? Allow yourself to sob; allow yourself to feel every emotion running through your body.

Visualize yourself drenched from this beautiful flowing natural source of comfort and love. Stay in that space for as long as you feel necessary.

Allow your mind to run; allow angry words and brokenhearted cries. Allow your tears to flow freely.

Now, when you feel the tears subsiding, notice how the weather's changed.
Is it bright with the new dawn breaking or cold and dreary? If it is the latter, move into your visualization more and allow your emotions, that are yours to feel, to present themselves to you, gently, uninhibited and free.
Once you see the brightness of the new day dawning, lift your face to the sky, allowing the new sun's rays to gently dry your tears. Reach your arms wide and smile through your tears if they are still flowing. Embrace what is rightfully yours; embrace your new self and your new found freedom. Do this every day until you feel ready to let go.

Letting Go Visualization

After the grieving visualization is full completed and you are relaxed and feel empowered (powered and motivated within your 'self'), visualize yourself standing on a rock ledge with the beautiful new dawn in front of you, with your cleansing meadow below. Notice on what side the meadow is to you...Is it to the left, right or straight down?

1 Again, raise your hands out wide and lifting your head to the sky, smile warmly and brightly. You may even see yourself laughing. After a few brief moments, then notice two Beings on either side of you.

These Beings are known universally as 'Children of the Feather' or 'Angels'. There is no need to visualize their faces. Just know that they are there in loving guidance and protection. Again, notice two other Beings, one in front, one behind you. These Beings can also be 'Children of the Feather' or simply others that you feel great peace and love from. These could be family members passed on or still here, friends, or your own spiritual guides.

2 Next, take a gentle step forward toward the edge of the cliff. Notice how the guides move in perfect unison with you, always guiding, always protecting and always loving.

3 Again, take another step towards the cliff edge. Notice the guides' constant movement and gentle watchfulness and reassurance of your movements and mannerisms.

4 Again take another step towards the cliff edge. Take five steps in total always looking ahead and feeling every emotion.

5 Next, closing your eyes, take another step and breathe, not deeply or shallowly, but more like sighing. A great release is taking place and sighing is your body's natural way of responding. Now smiling, open your eyes.

6 Become aware that you are hovering a foot away from the cliff edge that is now behind you. Notice the guides nod and smile with appreciation of the recognition of freedom that spreads across your face.

7 Visualize the above scene at least once every day until you feel ready, powerful and secure in your choices and your courage.

8 Now, breathe in deeply and look around you. What is the scenery like? Are your guides still with you? Are you hovering higher than the cliff or below?

9 Feel what direction you would like to take, left, right, towards the dawn or towards the cliff face? Notice your heart rhythm.

Is it a steady rhythm or is it racing? Remember it is your choice which direction you would like to take. There is no right direction or wrong direction. There is no backwards or past, or future, only this instant. It is your choice.

Nicole.

A Question Asked

Here's something to ponder on - and no doubt over analyze Nicole. I'm going to leave you tonight with this last thought.

What if all this wasn't real?

What if every single person you came into contact with today were you in a different disguise? What if all those people you see and converse with were just various energies of your OWN personality?

(laughs)

Now THAT'S got you thinking hasn't it?

Prologue

It's been almost 14 years since Jason 'Passed through Time'. I won't say it has been easy, far from it. However, in having our conversations together, he has allowed me to 'choose' not to fear life, but embrace it and live it fully so that I will find and remember the realization of Who I Am and Why I Am.

I urge everyone who has had a loved one 'Pass through Time' to speak of them and most importantly, with them.

There is no special gift involved. Only the love that you have for one another is all you need. Love is stronger than anything that we will ever 'choose' to experience.

Speak with them, just in your mind. Tell them what you always wanted to say and share with them. Hold them close to your heart and the connection with them will become instant.

I know if everybody allowed themselves to reconnect with their loved ones who have passed before them, we will personally and universally become better people, a better race and a more loving, connected world.

As I have spoken with Jay, he has allowed me to realize that 'death' is nothing to fear, or speak about in hushed whispers, but can be spoken about honestly, truthfully and with no judgment.
With what Jay has described, 'Death' no longer needs to be 'the final frontier' but something - an energy structure we can learn from and grow through - an exciting adventure, filled with love and peace-filled hope.

My only wish for you as you have read these words of Jay's is that your remembrance and reconnection with your loved ones become stronger and joyous and is now unbreakable from the 'distance of death'.

All is One, is One.

squishy hugs

Nicole Suzanne Brown November, 2012

Jay - 1997

About the Author – Nicole Suzanne Brown

Nicole Suzanne Brown, lived in sunny Queensland all her life until moving to a very small cold country town of New South Wales, and still is confused by the choice to this day as the sun is always calling her. Small in stature but big in personality, she has lived in New York, the United Kingdom, spent time in an Indian Ashram and gets itchy feet every time she glances at her Passport. She is the creator and Editor in Chief of Spiritual Wisdom Magazine, a best-selling monthly magazine (also available as an e-zine) released January, 2013. When not writing you can find her contemplating her navel, somewhere, in some part of the world.

You can connect with her online at -

www.ingramcontent.com/pod-product-compliance
Lightning Source LLC
Chambersburg PA
CBHW060459010526
44118CB00018B/2469